THE FAITHFUL VIRGINS

The Other Voice in Early Modern Europe:
The Toronto Series, 104

E. POLWHELE

The Faithful Virgins

Edited by

ANN HOLLINSHEAD HURLEY

Iter Press
NEW YORK | TORONTO

2023

Printed in the United States of America

978-1-64959-097-8 (paper)
978-1-64959-098-5 (pdf)
978-1-64959-099-2 (epub)

Library of Congress Cataloging-in-Publication Data
Names: Polwhele, Elizabeth, author. | Hurley, Ann, 1947- editor.
Title: The faithful virgins / E. Polwhele ; edited by Ann Hollinshead Hurley.
Description: New York : Iter Press, 2023. | Series: The other voice in early modern Europe. The Toronto series ; 104 | Includes bibliographical references and index. | Summary: "The first printed edition of Polwhele's first play, -Faithful Virgins-, a tragicomedy apparently performed in London by the Duke's Company ca. 1669-1671, until now extant only in an unsigned manuscript in the Bodleian Library at Oxford University. The introduction to this modern-spelling edition discusses the play in terms of radical changes in English stage practices following the restoration of the monarchy after England's civil war and situates Polwhele's play within the social and political life of seventeenth-century London"-- Provided by publisher.
Identifiers: LCCN 2023022308 (print) | LCCN 2023022309 (ebook) | ISBN 9781649590978 (paperback) | ISBN 9781649590985 (pdf) | ISBN 9781649590992 (epub)
Subjects: LCGFT: Drama.
Classification: LCC PR3619.P67 F35 2023 (print) | LCC PR3619.P67 (ebook) | DDC 822.4--dc23/eng/20230609
LC record available at https://lccn.loc.gov/2023022308
LC ebook record available at https://lccn.loc.gov/2023022309

Cover Illustration
Called Anne Bracegirdle (Anne Bracegirdle, 1671–1748; actress). Artist unknown. Courtesy of the Garrick Club, London.

Cover Design
Maureen Morin, Library Communications, University of Toronto Libraries.

For Rodger Lawrence Hurley
and
Kevin James Shields

Contents

Acknowledgments

Not surprisingly for a project like this, with little available in the way of primary sources, a significant amount of support is essential. Accordingly, I am indebted to a number of individuals and institutions. Most important are the resources of Wagner College. Dennis Schaub, dean of the Wagner College Horrmann Library, and his reference and interlibrary loan staff provided quick, informed, and professional support throughout this project. Our highly skilled librarian Catherine Perkins was essential to me in assisting with digital formatting. Over the years, the members of the Faculty Personnel Committee of Wagner College provided financial resources, and the College Scholarship Circle at Wagner College was a valuable testing ground for much of my initial writing.

Other institutions were vital in helping me to develop the skills to carry out this research. A National Endowment for the Humanities Summer Stipend initiated my work, and the staffs of the Folger Shakespeare Library and the Bodleian Library at Oxford sustained it. Heather Wolfe of the Folger Library, an insightful reader of obscure scripts, gave the Rare Book School paleography seminar that clarified my transcription of Polwhele's play, and other courses at the Rare Book School at the University of Virginia extended my understanding of manuscript work. In addition, the English language editor of The Other Voice series, Elizabeth Hageman, provided essential guidance throughout the preparation of this text, and I am indebted to her for her astute attention to detail and her well-tested patience.

I am even more deeply indebted to my colleagues. Chanita Goodblatt worked tirelessly with me over the years as we both sought support for projects involving women writers of the early modern period. Her 2017 panel at the annual meeting of the Renaissance Society of America introduced Polwhele to the editors of The Other Voice series and thus made publication of this play a reality. The members of the English Department at Wagner, who were subjected to too many descriptions of my endlessly ongoing research, are the best of friends as well as scholarly supporters. Felicia Ruff and Theresa McCarthy, from the Theatre Department at Wagner, gave essential assistance to my teaching and performance understanding of this play. Most importantly, I owe to my Wagner colleagues Erica Johnson, Chris Hogarth, Anne Schotter, and in particular, Margarita Sanchez, Rosemary Anarumo, and Susan Bernardo my gratitude for their immediate and then ongoing support at a time of crisis. Without them and the other members of my faculty family this book would not have been finished.

Finally, this volume is dedicated to the two men who have supported, proofread, discussed, critiqued, travelled with, loved, encouraged, and been present for me through the many years of its production. For Rodger Lawrence

Hurley (1940–2010), my husband, and Kevin James Shields, my husband of recent years, my gratitude and my deepest love.

Illustrations

Abbreviations

ESTC	English Short Title Catalogue
ODNB	*Oxford Dictionary of National Biography* (online version)
OED	*Oxford English Dictionary* (online version)
Wing	*Short-Title Catalogue of Books Printed in England . . . 1641–1700.* 2nd ed. Edited by Donald Wing et al. 3 vols. New York: Modern Language Association of America, 1994–98.

Introduction

The Other Voice

The Faithful Virgins by E. Polwhele, written ca. 1669–1671, is a rewarding play for the study of texts, women playwrights of that period, performance expectations, and the theatrical practices of the first theaters established under Charles II, who returned to the English throne on May 29, 1660. As an early Restoration play, it is particularly useful to students and scholars in demonstrating this playwright's understanding of theatrical performance demands and, especially, audience expectations.

The plot of the play can be briefly summarized. It concerns three "faithful virgins": Umira, Merantha, and Erasila. The play opens with Umira and Merantha weeping before a hearse containing the remains of a young lord, Philammon, whom they both loved. There is, in addition, a lustful Duke who betrays his wife, Isabella, by attempting to seduce Umira, whom the Duchess Isabella subsequently seeks to murder. Meanwhile, the third virgin and sister of Philammon, Erasila, has disguised herself as a page to get closer to Statenor, the lord she loves, and suffers accordingly. While the ending of the play, with its requisite deaths, might imply a tragedy, the handling of the characters, sometimes verging on the satiric, is often comic.

In a conventional introduction such as this, one might next expect an answer to the usual initial question, "Who was E. Polwhele?" There is some ambiguity about this (see the end of this introduction), and thus the answer: we do not know. Her play has been hidden in the archives of the Bodleian Library at Oxford for nearly four centuries, only occasionally noted and still largely unread. Those few who have commented on it gave it little credit and essentially wrote off its playwright as a young, inexperienced writer, somewhat star-struck and with little promise as a serious author.[1] They saw little in the play itself and thus found it unrewarding for scholarship and certainly unfit for print.

This neglect can be partially attributed to a subtle tendency to see women playwrights as less experienced than their male contemporaries, even when such an assessment is excused, somewhat condescendingly, because of the limitations of female education and the assumed social exclusion of women from theatrical circles. These assumptions are then read back into female-authored plays—seeing

1. See, for example, the remark that Polwhele's play "never attained the dignity of print" in Montague Summers, *The Playhouse of Pepys* (1935; repr., New York: Humanities Press, 1964), 338–41. See also Judith Milhous and Robert D. Hume, introduction to *The Frolicks; or, The Lawyer Cheated (1671)*, by E. Polwhele (Ithaca, NY: Cornell University Press, 1977), 13–54, who see the author of this play as "a novice writer" (43).

them as unaccomplished due to their authors' limitations, or accomplished in spite of them. Women playwrights were seen as lacking the opportunities to become proficient in their craft and also as conditioned to be wary of the stigma of putting oneself at risk of the notoriety often attached to female authorship. The disparaging terms used for Aphra Behn and Margaret Cavendish are said to be representative, and the reluctance of Katherine Philips to publish is often cited as again suggestive of female self-censuring—a wariness born out of the familiar alignment of female actors and, by extension, female playwrights with prostitutes. Much of this stereotyping of women playwrights as being denied the advantages of their male counterparts and therefore less competent certainly arises from the attitudes of their contemporaries. But some of it also drifts into contemporary scholarship.[2]

To answer, then, the question of who was "E. Polwhele" requires turning away from the conventional initial focus on gender as biography ("Life") and turning instead to gender as situated in the context of the play itself ("Works"). What were the theatrical conditions out of which this play emerged? How well does the play negotiate them? What does it contribute to our understanding of early Restoration drama? And what kind of a female author does the play itself construct? Questions like these, with a focus on how radically the Restoration stage had altered theatrical conventions, audience expectations, and even the nature of the physical stage itself, and how well the play meets these conditions, can ultimately yield a more complete understanding of who E. Polwhele might have been and how to assess her talent.

Polwhele's Play in Its Historical Context: The Return of Charles II and the Early Restoration Period

The years of the early Restoration (1660–1670) mark radical social and political changes from the England of Shakespeare's era and from the recent Commonwealth period (1649–1660), including important changes in the nature of theatricality. In 1660, Charles II, son of Charles I, who had been executed in 1649, was invited by Parliament to restore the Stuart monarchy to the English throne. He was received in London with public celebrations, bonfires, bell ringing, pageantry, and much

2. For a useful summary of seventeenth-century attitudes and contemporary scholarship on women writers and playwrights, see Laura Lunger Knoppers, "Introduction: Critical Framework and Issues," in *The Cambridge Companion to Early Modern Women's Writing*, ed. Laura Lunger Knoppers (Cambridge: Cambridge University Press, 2009), 1–18. For more specific studies of the reputation of women playwrights, see Catherine Gallagher, "Who Was That Masked Woman? The Prostitute and the Playwright in the Comedies of Aphra Behn," *Women's Studies* 15, no. 1–3 (1988): 23–42, https://doi.org/10.1080/00497878.1988.9978715; Jacqueline Pearson, *The Prostituted Muse: Images of Women and Women Dramatists, 1642–1737* (New York: St. Martin's Press, 1988), 1–23, 119–42; and Wendy Wall, *The Imprint of Gender: Authority and Publication in the English Renaissance* (Ithaca, NY: Cornell University Press, 1993).

enthusiasm, signifying the nation's relief at the end to the religious rigidity and antitheatricality of the Commonwealth period. That is, the pageantry accompanying Charles II's entrance into London and his coronation on April 23, 1661, signaled not only a return of monarchy but also a restoration of the theatricality that had traditionally accompanied such celebrations. Samuel Pepys, whose *Diary* record of the coronation describes the immediacy and enthusiasm of the moment, accentuates this theatricality, which would become a defining element of Charles II's reign:

> And a pleasure it was to see [Westminster] Abbey raised in the middle, all covered with red, and a throne . . . and footstoole on the top of it. And all the officers of all kinds, so much as the very fidlers, in red vests. At last comes in the Deane and prebends of Westminster, with the Bishops (many of them in cloth-of-gold Copes); and after them the nobility, all in their parliament-robes, which was a most magnificent sight. Then the Duke [of York], and the King with a scepter (carried by my Lord of Sandwich) and Sword and mond [orb] before him, and the crowne too. The King in his robes, bare-headed, which was very fine.[3]

In the context of *The Faithful Virgins*, this passage and others like it that signify Pepys's delight in the return of pageantry are particularly important because the coronation of Charles II marked not just the return of the monarchy but also the reopening of theater, closed for the past eighteen years. It also signaled a monarch whose pleasure in and knowledge of theater was to be a defining element of his reign. In fact, in the first year of his reign, the king issued two warrants for the establishment of what were to become the two primary theatrical companies for the next decade. These warrants were granted to two courtiers, Thomas Killigrew and William Davenant, who, following Continental models, established two indoor London theaters in leased tennis courts, a significant change in theatrical space that in turn dictated changes in staging, performance, and even the shaping of the audience, which would directly influence playwrights like Polwhele.[4] A second important innovation from Charles II was his edict commanding theatrical companies to use women actors for all female parts. The title of Polwhele's play, *The Faithful Virgins*, clearly reflects the playwright's willingness to adapt to this edict.[5]

3. Samuel Pepys, *The Diary of Samuel Pepys*, ed. Robert C. Latham and William Matthews, vol. 2, *1661* (London: G. Bell and Sons Ltd., 1970), 83–84.

4. The warrants, issued in the summer of 1660, are cited in Judith Milhous and Robert D. Hume, eds., *A Register of English Theatrical Documents, 1660–1737*, vol. 1 (Carbondale: Southern Illinois University Press, 1991), 2, 5.

5. For the order for women actors, see Charles II's formal statement as part of that patent to Killigrew that "we do . . . permit and give leave that all the women's parts to be acted in either of the . . . two companies for the time to come . . . be performed by women," cited in Jonathan Bate and Russell Jackson, eds., *Shakespeare: An Illustrated Stage History* (Oxford: Oxford University Press, 1996), 49.

Although the copy of the license of Henry Herbert, Master of the Revels, attached to the title page of the manuscript of *The Faithful Virgins* cites it as a "Tragedy," it is difficult to read the play as if composed with totally serious intent. More likely it was a version of romantic tragicomedy, a popular genre of this period.[6] Several scenes in the play can only be read as satiric, and some requisite dead figures at its end are posed in such a way as to emphasize the melodramatic aspect of spectacle. None of the characters arouse our full sympathy, nor are pity and fear, the classically moving tragic emotions, called for in any affective way. And, finally, and perhaps most pertinently, one character, the Duke, is handled in such a way as to point to some amusingly risky parallels between him and the reigning monarch, Charles II.[7] It would seem that, in this play, Polwhele is manipulating and commenting on the theatrical conventions of the day in a comic, almost satiric way, and with much energy and wit.

Polwhele's Play in the Context of the Changing Restoration Stage

In appointing Killigrew and Davenant, courtiers who had been in exile with him on the Continent, as managers of his two designated theatrical companies, Charles encouraged London theater to import some of the theatrical conventions that he and his courtiers had been exposed to while in exile.[8] These included not only a shift from open-air theaters, like the Globe, to indoor performance spaces, but also increased use of changeable scenery, such that scene changes were effected by shutters set in up to five grooves and by matching wings, also set in grooves. Moveable scenery included elaborately painted background sets that could be revealed or hidden when the shutters were manipulated. One of the most frequent uses of such scenery was the back-shutter discovery scene, in which a pair of painted shutters was suddenly withdrawn to reveal a farther part of the stage, complete with its own scenic backing. Moreover, the use of such moveable scenery clarified entrances and exits so that actors no longer needed to leave the stage to signify a change of scene. Although painted scenery had been seen in pre-Restoration court theatricals, the general public probably did not see such moveable

6. Romantic tragicomedy is a theatrical genre that blends aspects of tragedy and comedy with subject matter that involves romantic interests. Popular in the seventeenth century both before and after the Restoration, in its later evolution it tended toward melodrama of a kind that may be found in Polwhele's play. For a discussion of the political uses of tragicomedy, see Nancy Klein Maguire, *Regicide and Restoration: English Tragicomedy, 1660–1671* (Cambridge: Cambridge University Press, 1992).

7. Milhous and Hume make a similar point in their discussion of this play in their introduction to the Cornell edition of *The Frolicks* (43).

8. Charles II had spent nine years of exile in France, the Dutch Republic, and the Spanish Netherlands. These years of exile influenced his love of theater and, in particular, the French stage, with its use of moveable scenery, stage, and flying machinery, and women actors for the female roles. Killigrew and Davenant also followed the French in taking over tennis courts for theatrical performances.

and painted scenery until 1661, when Davenant's *Siege of Rhodes* was performed at his Lincoln's Inn Fields Theater.[9] Whereas actors of pre–Civil War generations performed on a platform stage, most frequently in the open air, Restoration actors performed on an apron stage that allowed for a scenic area upstage, sometimes in front of a curtain, thus putting the actors closer to the audience. Adding to the effect of perspective was the framing of the whole with an elaborate proscenium arch that separated the stage from the auditorium and thus allowed for considerable visual embellishment as well as an enhanced perception of depth.

As these theaters evolved, they also came to include stage machinery, like ceiling features where flying equipment could be located. Doors on each side of the stage allowed for entrances and exits such that, again, an actor no longer needed to leave the stage and then reenter to indicate scene changes. The audience was seated either in the pit or in galleries or boxes at the front and sides of the stage. Because the stage as a whole was smaller than the open-air theaters of Shakespeare's time, the audience was in close proximity to the players and could, and often did, comment to and about them.[10] As these were indoor theaters, lighting was also important. Though primitive, largely achieved via wax candles in sconces or chandeliers, the lighting was sufficient and differed significantly from our present day in that it illuminated the audience as well as the stage, and thus contributed to the greater intimacy of the Restoration theater in contrast to its open-air predecessors.

Moreover, elaborate stage effects not only marked a significant change in Restoration staging from its pre–Civil War predecessors, but they also generated a new kind of audience, one that would be attentive to stage scenery and spectacle—the more lavish the better. The stage directions that open Davenant's 1667 production of Shakespeare's *The Tempest* (see Fig. 1), for example, illustrate well how Restoration playwrights anticipated and delivered on such expectations.

9. Dawn Lewcock, *Sir William Davenant, the Court Masque, and the English Seventeenth-Century Scenic Stage, c. 1605–c. 1700* (Amherst, NY: Cambria Press, 2008), 1, 113.

10. For further discussion of Restoration staging and dramaturgy, see Eleanore Boswell, *The Restoration Court Stage, 1660–1702: With a Particular Account of the Production of Calisto* (1932; repr., New York: Barnes and Noble, 1966); Edward A. Langhans, "Theatre," in *The Cambridge Companion to English Restoration Theatre*, ed. Deborah Payne Fisk (Cambridge: Cambridge University Press, 2000), 1–18; Edward A. Langhans, "The Post-1660 Theatres as Performance Spaces," in *A Companion to Restoration Drama*, ed. Susan J. Owen (Oxford: Blackwell, 2001), 3–18; Derek Hughes, *English Drama, 1660–1700* (Oxford: Clarendon Press, 1996); Robert D. Hume, *The Development of English Drama in the Late Seventeenth Century* (Oxford: Clarendon Press, 1976); Richard Leacroft, *The Development of the English Playhouse* (Ithaca, NY: Cornell University Press, 1973); Lewcock, *Sir William Davenant*; Judith Milhous and Robert D. Hume, *Producible Interpretation: Eight English Plays 1675–1707* (Carbondale: Southern Illinois University Press, 1985); William Van Lennep, Emmett L. Avery, and Arthur Scouten, eds., *The London Stage, 1660–1800*, Part 1, *1600–1700* (Carbondale: Southern Illinois University Press, 1965); and Richard Southern, *Changeable Scenery: Its Origin and Development in the British Theatre* (London: Faber and Faber, 1952).

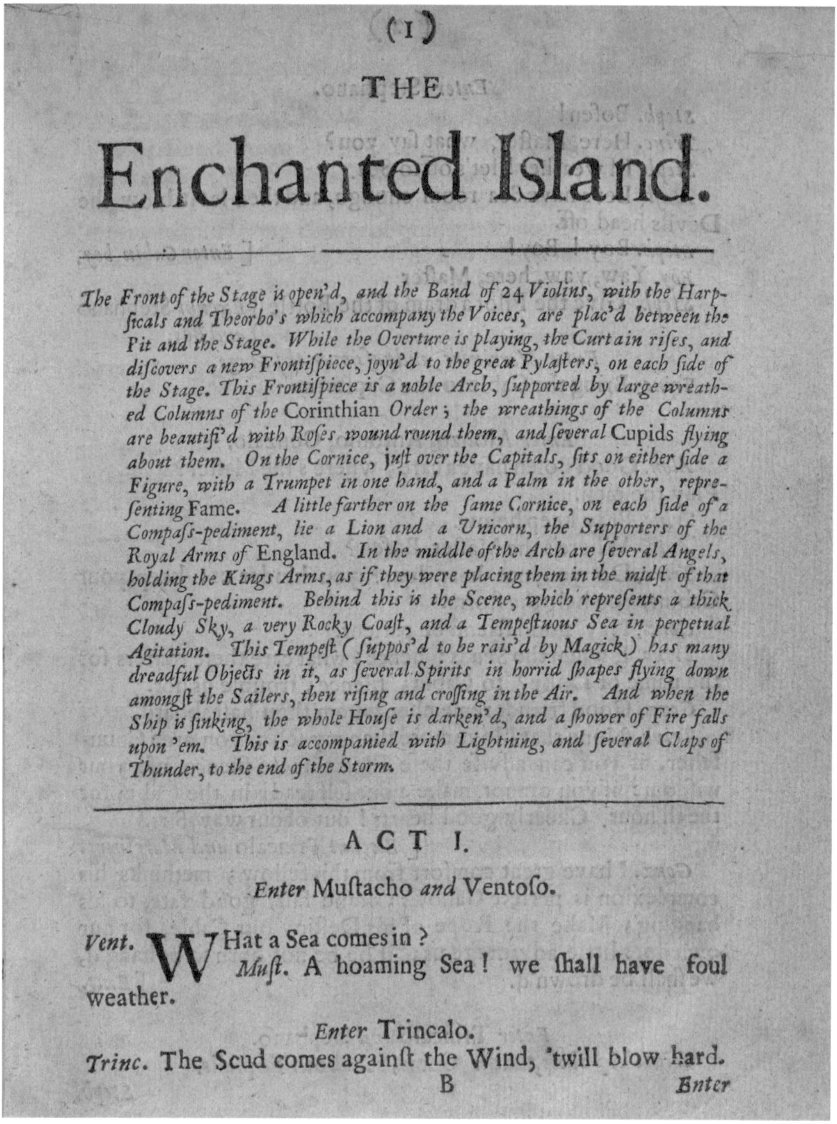
(1)

THE

Enchanted Island.

The Front of the Stage is open'd, and the Band of 24 *Violins, with the Harpſicals and Theorbo's which accompany the Voices, are plac'd between the Pit and the Stage. While the Overture is playing, the Curtain riſes, and diſcovers a new Frontiſpiece, joyn'd to the great Pylaſters, on each ſide of the Stage. This Frontiſpiece is a noble Arch, ſupported by large wreathed Columns of the* Corinthian *Order; the wreathings of the Columns are beautifi'd with Roſes wound round them, and ſeveral* Cupids *flying about them. On the Cornice, juſt over the Capitals, ſits on either ſide a Figure, with a Trumpet in one hand, and a Palm in the other, repreſenting* Fame. *A little farther on the ſame Cornice, on each ſide of a Compaſs-pediment, lie a Lion and a Unicorn, the Supporters of the Royal Arms of* England. *In the middle of the Arch are ſeveral Angels, holding the Kings Arms, as if they were placing them in the midſt of that Compaſs-pediment. Behind this is the Scene, which repreſents a thick Cloudy Sky, a very Rocky Coaſt, and a Tempeſtuous Sea in perpetual Agitation. This Tempeſt (ſuppos'd to be rais'd by Magick) has many dreadful Objects in it, as ſeveral Spirits in horrid ſhapes flying down amongſt the Sailers, then riſing and croſſing in the Air. And when the Ship is ſinking, the whole Houſe is darken'd, and a ſhower of Fire falls upon 'em. This is accompanied with Lightning, and ſeveral Claps of Thunder, to the end of the Storm.*

ACT I.

Enter Muſtacho *and* Ventoſo.

Vent. WHat a Sea comes in?

Muſt. A hoaming Sea! we ſhall have foul weather.

Enter Trincalo.

Trinc. The Scud comes againſt the Wind, 'twill blow hard.

B *Enter*

Figure 1. *The Enchanted Island.* Opening stage direction for the Dryden, Davenant, and Shadwell production of Shakespeare's *The Tempest.* Folger Shakespeare Library, Washington, DC. S2945 B, fol. 1r.

The license attached to Polwhele's play states that it was licensed for performance by "the Duke's Company of Actors," that is by Davenant's company, which was noted by Pepys and others as initially more cognizant of Continental theatrical staging than was its competitor, Killigrew's King's Men, then acting at the Theatre Royal on Bridges Street.[11] Davenant's converted tennis court theater, Lincoln's Inn Fields, opened in 1661, was the first public theater to use changeable scenery.[12] Moreover, Davenant's company was known to have been more likely to perform plays by less well-known playwrights than was Killigrew's, as Killigrew had inherited most of the performance scripts from the pre–Civil War King's Company.[13] Polwhele's play, coming from a relatively unknown playwright, would thus have been more likely to have been selected by Davenant, even if we did not already have Herbert's license corroborating this fact.

More pertinently, Davenant's personal history with court masques may also have played a role in his decision to produce Polwhele's play.[14] In his own playwriting, he had adapted the masque spectacle from an earlier masque to the public stage in the staging of his *Siege of Rhodes*, as evidenced in the 1663 printed version, and masque and spectacle were thus associated with his theatrical company.[15] As almost all of act 3 of Polwhele's *The Faithful Virgins* takes the form of both antimasque and masque, her play is thus consistent with the influence of masque and with the developing genre of rhymed verse drama of the kind that would have appealed to Davenant. His background and experience with Restoration changes in stage conventions is thus pertinent to our understanding *The Faithful Virgins* in the context of the shift from platform to scenic staging.

Davenant's pre-Restoration experience with masque as both playwright and producer involved collaboration with the knowledgeable set designers Inigo Jones and John Webb.[16] From 1631, when he was appointed by Charles I to replace Ben Jonson as poet of masques, until his death in 1668, Davenant gained and displayed the technical and mechanical expertise associated with masques. His 1661 production of *The Siege of Rhodes*, for example, brought Charles II to the public

11. Hughes, *English Drama*, 1–2.

12. Derek Hughes, *The Theatre of Aphra Behn* (Hampshire: Palgrave, 1988), 12.

13. Lewcock, *Sir William Davenant*, 112.

14. A masque was a courtly entertainment involving dancing, singing, instrumental music, song, and acting, plus elaborate stage design featuring architectural motifs, machinery, and often innovative dramatic effects. It was designed to entertain and to awe but also had moral, social, and political allegorical import. It was usually preceded by an "antimasque," a comic or grotesque dance that was transformed by the masque that followed it into propriety and order, usually by the king, or patron's, active presence.

15. For an extended discussion of the use of masque in Davenant's plays, see Maguire, *Regicide and Restoration*, 83–93.

16. For Jones and his role in masques, see Stephen Orgel and Roy C. Strong, *Inigo Jones: The Theatre of the Stuart Court*, 2 vols. (London: Sotheby Parke Bernet; Berkeley: University of California Press, 1973). See also John Newman, "Jones, Inigo (1573–1652)," in *ODNB*, ed. Lawrence Golden (Oxford: Oxford University Press, 2004), https://doi.org/10.1093/ref:odnb/15017; and John Bold, "Webb, John (1611–1672)," in *ODNB*, ed. Lawrence Golden (Oxford: Oxford University Press, 2004), https://doi.org/10.1093/ref:odnb/28922.

theater for the first time, thus verifying the royal as well as popular appreciation of plays with masque elements. We have relatively few depictions of how these performances appeared on stage, although the sketches in the Devonshire Collection at Chatsworth House give us some idea of how these might have appeared to contemporary audiences (see chatsworth.org). Their effect can also be read in the comments of playgoers like Pepys, who saw *Hamlet* in 1661 and approved the production of that play "as done with scenes."[17] And in Richard Flecknoe's praise of Davenant's productions as having "arrived to the height of magnificence," it is apparent that audience attention had shifted from the verbal to the visual.[18] When Polwhele came to write her *Faithful Virgins* sometime in the 1660s, then, she was faced with constructing a play that emerged as much from contemporary dramatic visual performances as from contemporary dramatic verbal texts.

Finally, the fact that we cannot find documentary evidence beyond that notation of the license does not negate the possibility that Polwhele's play was performed. As Robert D. Hume notes, "Performance records for the professional theatres in London remain radically incomplete until 1705."[19] Thus it is impossible to conclude that absence from these records means that Polwhele's play was not performed. What is particularly important is that even without definitive performance evidence, we can still conclude that Polwhele's play would have been radically different from pre-Restoration drama in staging and in promoting a more directly engaged audience response.

Applying this focus to a reading of Polwhele's *Faithful Virgins*, then, we might look at what the play itself can tell us about how it may have appealed to early Restoration audiences. Most pertinently, a close reading demonstrates that Polwhele was composing her play with the new performative values of the Restoration stage in mind. Act 1, for example, opens, as mentioned earlier, with a "discovery scene." One of the "faithful virgins," Merantha, is seen "weeping," and the second virgin, Umira, then enters. The stage directions read, "A hearse *discovered*" (my emphasis), making explicit that the playwright intended this opening to be performed as a scenic disclosure, something that had been done in the pre-Restoration era, but which was handled quite differently after 1660, when shutters and painted scenery could be employed to enhance both the perspective and the emotional qualities of the drama. In his discussion of the change in the handling of discovery scenes, Tim Keenan comments on the difference between the platform stage and the scenic stage with respect to this theatrical device: "Dramatic as they undoubtedly could be, . . . discoveries were . . . a direct inheritance from the old platform stage. Platform stage discoveries, however, were less frequent [and]

17. See entries for August 24, 1661, and August 21, 1661, in Pepys, *Diary*.

18. Richard Flecknoe, "A Short Discourse of the English Stage," in *Love's Kingdom* (London: R. Flecknoe, 1664), 11.

19. Robert D. Hume, "Theatre Performance Records in London, 1660–1705," *The Review of English Studies* 67 (June 2016): 468–95, https://doi.org/10.1093/res/hgv128.

tended to be brief, owing to unfavorable sight lines."[20] Keenan further observes that scenic stage settings, in contrast to platform stage settings, were often used to reveal settings with large props. In Polwhele's play, the opening discovery scene features a "hearse," possibly painted but also possibly a large prop that would return in several scenes to follow. (Thomas Porter's 1662 *The Villain* uses a hearse, suggesting this as a familiar prop.) Davenant also had used this new handling of the discovery scene in his own plays, and Keenan's research shows that while only 30 percent of known Globe plays used the discovery scene, at least 68 percent of the plays performed at Davenant's Lincoln's Inn Fields Theater used the new form of discovery; several of these used it more than once.[21] If Polwhele's *Faithful Virgins* used the new form of discovery scene, it would have called for shutters to disclose the scene and painted scenery to enhance the dramatic effect of sorrow and mourning. At the conclusion of this opening scene in act 1, the stage direction between lines 52 and 53 reads, "The hearse is *shut* in" (my emphasis), thus again suggesting that Polwhele's play is inviting the new scenic stage device of shutters and painted scenery.

For the remainder of act 1, scene changes are accomplished in the usual way, as indicated by the use of the stage direction *Exeunt omnes*. At the end of the act, however, Polwhele introduces a "dumb show," which includes the direction, "A temple *discovered*" (my emphasis), thus giving the audience an opportunity to enjoy the effects of spectacle, another attribute of Restoration theatricality.[22] While dumb shows were a feature of pre-Restoration drama, *Hamlet*'s mouse-trap play being the obvious example,[23] the use of the shutters and painted scenery made the visual appeal of these plays a new element to be noted and appreciated. Moreover, this dumb show, which features that "temple" before which a betrothal scene is silently acted out, seems designed to dramatically alter the mood of the previous somber scene in which the "faithful virgin" Erasila, disguised as the page Floradine, has been lamenting her unrequited love for Statenor, the courtier she serves. The discovery scene of that disclosed temple, when enhanced by painted scenery, makes a strikingly opulent visual commentary on the contrast of the lone character, Floradine, with the more crowded community celebration scene of betrothal.

More subtly, a second contrast might also have been made possible by the conjunction of discovery scene and dumb show. That is, the Duke is being betrothed to Isabella, who has just been seen rejecting her previous lover, Cleophon, and whom the Duke will, in turn, subsequently betray. An excessively lavish temple (achievable through the use of changeable scenery in the new scenic stage)

20. Tim Keenan, *Restoration Staging, 1660–74* (London: Routledge, 2017), 10.

21. Keenan, *Restoration Staging*, 176–77.

22. A dumb show is a dramatic action presented on stage without words, rather like mime, usually to summarize or comment on the main action.

23. See *Hamlet* 3.2.87–258.

might make a foreshadowing visual comment on the excessively lascivious nature of the Duke, and thus also the potential unreliability of events to come. Moreover, Davenant was known to reuse such props in the plays his company presented. As audiences grew to recognize these when used for spectacular effect, it is perhaps possible that a prop that was thus repurposed would carry with it some of the implications of its previous use. The new audience of the Restoration, increasingly trained to appreciate the spectacle involved in scenes like this conclusion to act 1 of Polwhele's play, would have been responsive to this use of props in a way that a pre-Restoration audience would not have been. Finally, if Polwhele's play was indeed performed by Davenant's company, a prop like the temple might also have been handled through the use of perspective effects. The Restoration audience was consciously alert to the ways in which things were perceived and apprehended in the special relationship between themselves and other objects, as Pepys's comments occasionally demonstrate.[24]

We do not have a complete record of specific stage props for either Davenant's or Killigrew's company, but we do know that Restoration staging was capable of elaborate effects. See, for example, the following description of one such spectacle, drawn from a performance later than Polwhele's play but nonetheless illustrative:

> The Clouds divide, and Juno appears in a Machine drawn by Peacocks while a Symphony is playing. It moves gently forward, and as it descends, it opens and discovers the Tail of the Peacock, which is so Large, that it almost fills the opening of the Stage between Scene and Scene.[25]

Davenant's company was invested in spectacle, and Polwhele's temple scene offered an opportunity for similar effect, although probably on a lesser scale.

Act 2 offers a similar opportunity to read Polwhele's play for how it suggests performance values aligned with the changing nature of the Restoration stage. It also opens with a discovery scene disclosing the hearse and thus returning viewers to the initial location. It closes with a stage direction given between lines 159 and 160 that is quite specific: "Enter Cleophon as in a grove looking about. On one side of it a cave [is] discovered." This shift reinforces the conjecture that a movement of shutters, rather than a cleared stage, marked the transition from one scene (the hearse) to another (the grove). That the cave is "discovered" further emphasizes that a movement of shutters to expose the cave must be involved. And again, painted scenery would reinforce the dramatic nature of the change.

24. Lewcock, *Sir William Davenant*, 238.

25. John Dryden, *Albion and Albanius*, quoted in Hughes, *Theatre of Aphra Behn*, 13. See also Fig. 1, p. 6.

Of some importance is our recognition that the goal here is not verisimilitude but entertainment. Scene changes with the movement of shutters and painted scenery, and the sequence and rapidity of scene changes themselves, all had begun to attract an interest not possible in pre-Restoration theater. The changes of scene became in fact an opportunity for commentary from the audience. Notably, the earliest comments are all from foreigners, suggesting the Continental audience's greater exposure to these effects, new to an English audience.[26]

The scene quickly becomes complicated by more calculated use of stage effects as two witches "enter" and "weave charms," though how they do this is not indicated. What does happen is that following one charm, "two spirits ascend in white, like nymphs" (stage direction between ll. 185 and 186). After some discourse, the next stage direction between lines 193 and 194 reads, "Witch stamps and spirits descend." The witch then states, with reference to additional "spirits," "I will conjure the spirits of the air / Straight to descend" (ll. 194–95). She exits, and the stage direction reads, "Thunder as in the air; as that eases, soft music and a song. Song ended and spirits in the shape of men and women descend and dance. Which being done, all vanish." There is more music, then "three aerial spirits descend" and, after more conversation, "ascend" and "vanish." There is thus much descending and ascending, suggesting the opportunity for stage machinery to again entertain the audience as well as further the plot.

Davenant's stage was equipped with the machinery to accomplish such action, and Polwhele's deliberate movement of her "spirits" again demonstrates an awareness of the entertainment value of such theatrical devices, as well as their value for the necessary complications of plot. In the 1660s, playgoing was still a new experience for many, and while much of the machinery used for these effects had been present in the aristocratic masques of earlier periods, they were new to the general Restoration audience and much to be marveled at. In this scene, Polwhele could well be described as responding to the desire for that kind of entertainment. Moreover, her pacing of the "descends" and "ascends" suggests an attentive awareness of when and how such audiences might react.

Act 3, in particular, evidences such performative intention, as almost the whole act is explicitly labeled a "masque," with accompanying dance and music throughout.[27] The first stage direction reads, "Two gentlemen discovered preparing seats for the Duke and Duchess," and the gentlemen's opening lines—"What

26. Some such seventeenth-century comments include the following: "The scene changes . . . are most ingeniously thought out and executed"; "the scenic area is quite open, with many scene changes and perspective views"; "the scenery is very light [and] capable of a great many changes." Quoted with attributions to Balthasar de Monconys (1663), Samuel Sorbière (1663), and Lorenzo Magalotti (1669), respectively, in Keenan, *Restoration Staging*, 65.

27. As stated earlier, a masque was usually preceded by an "antimasque," a comic or grotesque dance that was transformed by the masque that followed into propriety and order, usually by the active presence of the masque's patron. In Polwhele's masque, the activating presence is the Duchess.

is't the masquers do present tonight?" / "Somewhat in virtue's praise not worth our sight"—set the tone, with "Virtue's disgraced; we should not use her name" thus setting up the antimasque's critical nature. With a "flourish," the onstage audience is seated, including the Duke, new Duchess, and various courtiers and attendants. The masque that follows immediately takes up the entirety of act 3.

Polwhele's handling of this masque is deft and carefully composed, suggesting a full awareness of masque traditions and their use in 1660s contemporary theater, particularly in the modifications of that tradition given the Continental experience of Charles II and his court. Again, Davenant's experience in the production of masques is evident here.[28] Moreover, a masque, whether presented as an isolated dramatic entertainment or as part of a play, implied a distinct moral purpose and was also a multimedia performance involving script, song, instrumental music, and dance. Its patterns, whether visual or verbal, had the dual purpose of moral instruction and commentary as well as entertainment. Masques could be serious or comic, and in their antimasque/masque combination were usually both. Polwhele's masque, given that it is played out through the entire act, is explicit in moving between these two poles of pointed commentary and amused or awed entertainment, thus calling attention to the new versatility of the Restoration stage.

"The Masque" (stage direction), actually the antimasque, opens with the introduction of a series of figures, all representative of various sins. The first is Detraction, a choice of word suggesting the opposite of "attraction," with the possible implication of damaged reputation, something that the stage Duke might well consider and upon which the current monarch might also reflect. As the masque progresses, Detraction is joined by Envy, Ambition, Lechery, and other sins, and it is notable that Polwhele has reversed the traditional order of their entrance, starting not with the usual, Pride, but with sins more pointedly applicable to her contemporary times. The comment of the licensers attached to the text of the play, that "Luxury" be substituted for "Lechery," implies that the authorities saw the potential for royal offense, given the well-known promiscuity of Charles II, and attempted to address it. (Whether or not this substitution was carried out in the play's performance is not possible to verify, but the fact that the licensers use the word "pronounced" in their recommendation makes clear that the spoken performance should correct the written script.)

The act continues, and the stage directions also continue to offer evidence that Polwhele's script was attentive to the resources of Davenant's stage and to the multimedia performances associated with this aspect of Restoration drama. Not only does an angel enter (the script does not say "ascend," but the possibility is there), but the script also calls for "song," "music," and "dance" with "swift measure." There are in fact two kinds of dances involved, one in the antimasque with

28. For a detailed study of Davenant's considerable experience with the design and presentation of masques, see Lewcock, *Sir William Davenant*, esp. chs. 2–5.

drunken revelers, and the other in the masque proper involving the appropriate virtues. We cannot know what specific technical methods might have supported this particular play, but Davenant's theater was intended to convert the resources used for court masques into the elaborate set designs that facilitated some of the most dramatic visual effects of the Restoration stage.[29] Dance in particular held much of the allegorical meaning implied by the masque tradition, and the painted scenery that would have accompanied Polwhele's masque could also signify meaning. Given her revision of the order in which the sins enter and the apparent awareness of the licensers' implicit moral criticism, it is more than likely that the conversion of the disorderly rabble of the specific sins (Detraction, Envy, etc.), accomplished as Chastity and Virtue seat themselves at the feet of the Duchess, is pointedly intentional. In any case, it is a risky aspect of the play but may well imply this playwright's level of confidence rather than youthful naivete.

Finally, as to audience response to the kind of theater for which Polwhele was writing, we have the contemporary accounts of Pepys but also the 1664 comments from the playwright Richard Flecknoe. "Our" theaters, he says, are "arriv'd to the height of magnificence. . . . They are excellent helps of the imagination, most grateful deceptions of sight, and graceful and becoming ornaments of the Stage, transporting you easily without lassitude from one place to another; or rather by a delightful Magick, whilst you sit still, does bring the place to you."[30]

While act 3 may be the most visually arresting part of the play thus far, acts 4 and 5, working together, bring a conclusion that again requires an awareness of Restoration staging to fully appreciate. Act 4 seems, at least initially, to require little in stage effects aside from one discovery scene again disclosing the hearse, but it does prepare for a tableau effect at the conclusion of the play in act 5. To that end, the dramatic nature of the conclusion of act 4 in setting up what is to follow is reinforced by its final stage direction: "The scene is closed." Evidently, Polwhele felt that this act, which dramatizes the nature of the Duchess's situation, needed to be explicitly concluded with shutters so that the opening of the climactic act 5 would be clearly distinguished from what had led up to it.

Nonetheless, act 5 opens apparently simply, with chairs being "set out upon the stage by pages." That Polwhele included the phrase "upon the stage" may imply her intention that these be available for the series of conversations that take place. There is no direction that these chairs be removed, but the conversations, involving a number of plot details, are soon supplanted by action as the Duke and Duchess quarrel and then leave the stage separately, each now plotting against the other.

29. Davenant's intention to incorporate the painted changeable scenery and machinery of the court masque and Continental traditions into his new theater is apparent from the agreement he signed in November 1660 with the actor-sharers and one "Harris . . . *Painter*" (my italics). The reference to the "painter," here and elsewhere, clearly indicates his commission of skilled labor for elaborately painted scenery. See Lewcock, *Sir William Davenant*, 117.

30. Flecknoe, "Short Discourse," 12.

That this second action supplants the first suggests that the script of the play allows for shutters to be used to separate and thus further articulate the two scenes.

The action then accelerates as the Duke enters accompanied by "three or four" courtiers, all, including the Duke, "disguised" (stage direction between ll. 82 and 83). A number of entrances and exits follow in fairly rapid succession as the various strands of the plot begin to come together, thus increasing audience awareness of impending tragedy until the actual killing begins, starting with the death of Umira and resulting in a significant pile of bodies on the stage. A stage direction between lines 253 and 354, "The attendants help with the dead bodies," brings the mayhem to a close. The sequence of suicides, murders, mistaken identities, and assassinations occurs so quickly that its speed can only have been intentional, thus serving to undercut any potential opportunity for the audience to identify with any one character or to experience any cathartic effect.

There is then a scene that one might describe as a bridge between the preceding violence and the tableau that will conclude the play. Cleophon (the sole remaining aristocratic courtier, thus now to become the new duke) gives explicit directions to the attendants as they leave the stage—"Your patience in the cloister I desire / Whist but a few short minutes I retire" (ll. 254–55)—implying that he has a particular plan and thus suggesting to the audience that the play does not end here with the deaths that would usually conclude a tragedy. Instead, there is an interlude that is opened with very explicit stage directions. These directions are unusually specific with respect to positioning, costume, music, and sound, all features that a Restoration audience was being conditioned to respond to and expect: "The Duchess [is] discovered on a couch in rich nightdress. Soft music and a song within. Song ended. One knocks." The scene is quite brief and, after some few lines of dialogue, closes as both characters exit. They then immediately enter again with what appears to be a carefully designed stage direction: "The curtain is let fall. Solemn music awhile as it is drawn up again. The music ceases. At one door, enter Cleophon and the Duchess. At the other the lords" (between ll. 264 and 265). The references to "doors" and a "curtain" allude to some of the distinguishing aspects of the Restoration scenic stage, but what is particularly interesting is the juxtaposition of these features with the earlier theatrical device of clearing the stage via exits to indicate scene changes. Polwhele may have intended that her staging, which blended both old and new in scene changes, make clear that Cleophon and the Duchess are now an on-stage audience for the ensuing tableau.[31] The stage directions between lines 266 and 267 for the tableau, seemingly carefully composed, read as follows:

31. A tableau, or *tableau vivant* (living picture), in theatrical terms was a stationary, posed set of silent unmoving figures, usually theatrically lit. These were often featured in royal entries or aristocratic weddings. There may be some intended irony here in that these figures are posed not for a marriage but in death.

> The scene opens discovering Umira, Merantha, and Erasila, like a woman in white—with sparkling wreaths or coronets upon their heads—dead on a couch. Statenor's head placed on Erasila's lap. At the other side of the scene, Trasilius and the Duke are laid.

The apparently careful orchestration of this quick series of brief scenes, from violence to interlude to tableau, could be highly effective in moving an audience from engagement with violence to a brief respite that indulges the senses of sight and sound and then delivers a fitting conclusion, both verbal and visual. That Polwhele sets up her conclusion using the full resources of new Restoration theatrical effects, including dramatic tableau, suggests a playwright whose knowledge of theater is well tuned to her times and audience.

A Textual Consideration of Polwhele's Faithful Virgins

The argument being made thus far, that *The Faithful Virgins* is a play that attends to the performance interests of the early Restoration stage, has been carried out with little attention to dating, genre, or interpretation of the text. Given that we have no verified date for the play, such considerations must necessarily be speculative. Nonetheless, we can make some conjectures as to whether the play was written in the early or late 1660s.

The possibility that it was composed in the early 1660s rests on the assumption that Polwhele may have been among the young, potentially professional playwrights whom Davenant initially commissioned since the repertory of pre-Restoration plays, including Shakespeare's, had been assigned to the rival King's Men.[32] That rather circular argument assumes that *The Faithful Virgins* was Polwhele's first play, although in fact it might not have been. In her dedicatory letter appended to the later play, *The Frolicks*, of 1671, she refers to "those who have seen my *Faithful Virgins* and my *Elysium*," implying at least one other play or masque from her pen, and using diction ("seen") appropriate to actual, and likely recent, performance.[33] We know that the theaters were closed during the Great Plague and Great Fire of 1665 and 1666, respectively. Thus, a post-1666 date seems more likely than one in the early 1660s. In their edition of *The Frolicks*, Judith Milhous and Robert D. Hume agree that *The Faithful Virgins* "was almost certainly given a professional production," and they date the play to ca. 1670.[34]

32. Lewcock, *Sir William Davenant*, 112. See also Milhous and Hume, introduction to *The Frolicks*, 40; Van Lennep, Avery, and Scouten, *London Stage*, 65; and Alfred Harbage, *Annals of English Drama, 975–1700*, 2nd ed. Revised by S. Schoenbaum (London: Methuen, 1964), 168–69.

33. For the letter, see p. 22.

34. Milhous and Hume, introduction to *The Frolicks*, 41.

Additionally, a late 1660s date is also implied by the few additional fragments we have from Polwhele's pen, all of which come after 1670. First, a teasingly suggestive autograph, "Elizabeth Polwheile [*sic*] Her Booke," appears on the title page of a recent find in the British Library.[35] Titled *The Gentlewomans Companion; or, A Guide to the Female Sex*, this volume correlates well with Polwhele's emphasis on female roles in both of her extant plays. The subtitle continues, "Containing Directions of Behaviour, in all Places, Companies, Relations, and Conditions, from Their Childhood down to Old Age." The author (or compiler) is "Hannah Woolley," and the publication date is 1673.

A second document is a broadside ballad printed in 1672 in praise of James, Duke of York, and signed "Mrs. E. P." The Royalist sentiments evident in the ballad give some slight evidence of Polwhele's politics and a fuller suggestion of her sense of entitlement in speaking her mind.[36] Again, the late 1660s and early 1670s seems to be the period of her literary activity, at least so far as we can tell, and thus an appropriate period in which to date *The Faithful Virgins.*

Turning now to the topic of genre, as has already been suggested *The Faithful Virgins* conforms well to what scholars have identified as the common attributes of early Restoration theater in the 1660s. That is, it shares with other plays of this period in its creation of roles for actresses, its handling of stage conventions as dictated by the new theatrical space, particularly the use of the scenic stage, and its emphasis on dance and music in its third act. Its verse meter, the rhymed couplet, is also consistent with the heroic plays popular in the 1660s. There is evidence that Charles II reinstituted this verse form by requesting that the playwright Roger Boyle, First Earl of Orrery, write a play in this meter (*The Generall*, 1661). Commenting on that choice of verse form, Boyle noted that he did so "because I found his majesty relished rather the French fashion of playes, than the English."[37] The "French fashion" alludes to the influence of Pierre Corneille on 1660s English drama, but the rhymed heroic play also had English sources in Fletcher's plays and those of Dryden. Themes of love and honor and the heroic hyperbole of *The Faithful Virgins* are thus consistent with many other plays of the early Restoration theater. Moreover, the self-sacrificing virgin lovers—Merantha, Umira, and Erasila—are hardly unique in this period. In fact, *The Faithful Virgins* fits well with more than one of the dominant 1660s genres, particularly the rhymed heroic drama of Orrery and Dryden, and the romantic intrigues of Sir Samuel Tuke's tragicomedy, *Adventures of Five Hours* (1663).

Where *The Faithful Virgins* differs from the plays of the early 1660s, however, is largely in its tone. Scholars point out that by the close of the 1660s, tragicomedy had run its course and was occasionally being mocked. The plays of Tuke,

35. BL C.194.a.1455. See further comments, p. 26, and also Fig. 7 in the Appendix.

36. See further comments, p. 25, and also Fig. 8 in the Appendix.

37. Quoted in Maguire, *Regicide and Restoration*, 55.

Orrery, and even Dryden, with their plots of intrigue or their rigorous codes of conduct, though still popular, no longer moved audiences in the same way.[38] As early as 1664, for example, Robert Howard rewrote his ending to *The Vestal Virgin*, turning it from a tragedy to a romantic tragicomedy so that it could be acted "the comical way."[39] And Aphra Behn in her prologue to *The Amorous Prince* in 1671 declared her play "Not serious, nor yet comick," an apt description that could apply equally well to *The Faithful Virgins*.[40] The most direct evidence of this shift in audience appreciation for heroic hyperbole to mockery of it is in Buckingham's 1671 *Rehearsal*, a satire which, although aimed primarily at Dryden, could be read as directed at other sententious plays as well. It clearly illustrates the reaction of contemporaries to the overblown rhetoric of the heroic play. Thus, *The Faithful Virgins*, read in this context, can take on a tone of amused self-mockery. Given the quasi-satirical handling of the Duke in act 3, such a tone might well have been intended by the playwright.

This is hardly to say that the play should be read entirely as satire. The three faithful virgins, Merantha, Umira, and Erasila, can be seen as exemplary figures, particularly in contrast to the male characters, and the tableau at the end that portrays their deaths could well be moving. Instead, given the unusual interaction among playwrights of this period, such that "in every successive season, recently popular types, devices, plots, characters, and titles appear in new combinations and permutations,"[41] inconstancy of tone throughout a single play is not unusual. John Banks's *The Innocent Usurper* (1694), for example, a historically focused play, has a closing tableau of posed bodies like those of *The Faithful Virgins*, but there the tone is decidedly more bathos than pathos.

Where inconsistency within *The Faithful Virgins* is of greatest interest, however, is in the handling of the female characters, as Polwhele is also a playwright who responded with insight to the other new shift of this period, championed by Charles II, to use actresses for all female roles, and her play can certainly be read to engage this new position of women in the theater. In fact, to give her play a title, "The Faithful Virgins," that emphasizes the dominance of women's roles, and to make those roles, both exemplary figures and villains, the dominant emphasis in the plot development of the play, is to join fully in this aspect of the new theater of the 1660s.

We know that in the 1660s women playwrights began to appear with some frequency. Katherine Philips's translation of Corneille's *La Mort de Pompée* dates from the early 1660s. It was performed in February of 1663 and printed in both

38. Hume, *Development of English Drama*, 290–92.

39. Robert Howard, *Four New Plays* (London: Henry Herringman, 1665), 233–43.

40. Dawn Lewcock, *Aphra Behn Stages the Social Scene in the Restoration Theatre* (Amherst, NY: Cambria Press 2008), 71.

41. Hume, *Development of English Drama*, 17.

London and Dublin in the spring of that same year. We know that Philips's *Horace*, completed by Sir John Denham, was performed at court on February 4, 1668, by the Lady Castlemaine, Duchess of Cleveland, and others, and then at the Theatre Royal on Bridges Street during the 1668/9 theatrical season.[42] *Marcelia* was also performed in 1669 by Killigrew's King's Men,[43] and Margaret Cavendish's closet dramas, not written to be performed on stage, were now being published. Female actors had also begun to appear on stage; an unidentified woman played the role of Desdemona for the King's Men in 1660, and she was followed by several now well-known figures including Nell Gwyn and Mary "Moll" Davis.[44] Moreover, when William Davenant died in 1668, his wife took over part of the management of his company, bringing female management to theatrical practice. Thus, the 1660s marked the start of the officially endorsed participation of women in English theater.

Polwhele's play makes explicit that the female virtue of fidelity is being celebrated in direct contrast to the behavior of the unfaithful Duke and several of the male courtiers. Several lines from the play, repeated at various intervals, accentuate the differences between female fidelity and male openness to betrayals and, more explicitly, contrast the fidelity women have to each other with the lesser fidelity of love between men and women. Statenor, for example, trying to persuade his sister, Umira, to leave off mourning the death of her lover, says of men, "Love in our [male] griefs can hold but little room, / When the effect that made us love is gone" (act 1, ll. 81–82), while a page, speaking of Statenor's sister, explains that a woman, "like a chaste and watchful vestal keeps / Alive that flame love kindled in her breast, / Where it can ne'r be quenched, nor once suppressed" (act 1, ll. 76–78). The phrase "watchful vestal" alludes briefly to the Roman context of faithful Vestal Virgins, thus elevating, without more overt usage of that phrase, the moral and spiritual position of the women of the play.[45]

Moreover, as the three women continue to demonstrate, their fidelity to each other is even stronger than heterosexual love. Thus, even though it is love for the male courtier Philammon that Merantha and Umira have in common, their bond to each other is stronger, as various scenes and speeches reiterate. Indeed, at the play's conclusion, Merantha commits suicide to follow the dying Umira

42. For further discussion of Philips's role in bringing new influences to the 1660s Restoration stage, see Catherine Cole Mambretti, "Orinda on the Restoration Stage," *Comparative Literature* 37, no. 3 (Summer 1985): 233–51, https://doi.org/10.2307/1771080.

43. Derek Hughes, "Public Drama," in *The Cambridge Companion to Early Modern Women's Writing*, ed. Laura Lunger Knoppers (Cambridge: Cambridge University Press, 2009), 261–63.

44. For more concerning women on stage, see Elizabeth Howe, *The First English Actresses: Women and Drama, 1660–1700* (Cambridge: Cambridge University Press, 1992).

45. In ancient Rome, these virgins kept vigil over the sacred flame of Vesta, goddess of the hearth, thus emphasizing their virginity as well as representing the continuing power of the sacred Roman Empire.

after a rather lengthy speech, which ends with these lines right before she stabs herself: "Dear virgin, as thy love was great to me, / Thus I express, mine was no less to thee" (act 5, ll. 170–71). As Alison Findlay observes, through the course of the play, "Philammon's absence is gradually replaced by female presence."[46] Thus, the whole play seems to be designed on at least one level to radically reverse the trope of female emotionality and wanton instability into female bonding and "faithfulness."

There is in this context, however, the problem of the Duchess, whose characterization seems rather inconsistent, particularly where her role in the masque as the traditional exemplary figure is rather at odds with her action later in the play. At some points, her scenes invoke her as a familiar whore figure—the woman betraying one man and then punished for that betrayal in being herself betrayed by another. While the audience is not encouraged to develop much sympathy for the Duchess, it would be an oversimplification to see her as exemplifying either passive femininity or the traditional whore figure in contrast to the faithful virgins who center the play. On the one hand, she appropriates a masculine mode of retaliation against the faithless Duke in hiring an assassin to successfully dispatch him. On the other, though she takes charge of her own future, she is still relying on the traditional female skills of sexual manipulation to motivate that assassin. The scene of her reclining on the couch at the end of the play in a "rich night dress" with "soft music and song" as she waits to reward her assassin/lover is clearly designed to reinforce that implication. Again, at one point in the play she acknowledges "shame" for her betrayal, even labeling that betrayal a "sin" (act 1, ll. 102–3), while in the same scene Cleophon laments, "Oh woman! Ever created to deceive" (l. 139). Cleophon also indicts the Duchess's masculine role in plotting the play's violent conclusion "as the cause of all the spoils" and as damnable for the very sins of betrayal and lust, saying of her "soul . . . you have none" (act 5, ll. 277, 283). Finally, her use as an exemplifying figure, whose very presence banishes the sins of the masque and receives in their stead the figures of Virtue and (a rather "disheveled"[47]) Chastity, is undercut when she is herself banished at the play's conclusion. That final indictment is, tellingly, played out in front of the tableau of the three faithful virgins, memorialized in honorable death.[48]

If the problem of the contradictory nature of the role of the Duchess cannot be fully resolved at the narrative level of the play, its metanarrative implications do yield some interesting possibilities for speculation about Polwhele's larger interest

46. Alison Findlay, "Licensed to Thrill: Early Restoration Drama," in *Women and Dramatic Production, 1550–1700*, ed. Alison Findlay and Stephanie Hodgson-Wright, with Gweno Williams (New York: Routledge, 2000), 138.

47. Act 3, stage direction, p. 55.

48. For further discussion of the complexities of the female role as embodied in the Duchess, see Findlay, "Licensed to Thrill," 133–39.

in the female role and its social and theatrical possibilities. Here, her awareness of the changed role of the Restoration audience, and particularly her boldness in engaging the figures of the Duke and Duchess, suggests a playwright whose same boldness implies a certain level of protected social status. It is not at all a stretch to see the figure of the Duke as constituting only minimally veiled glances at the behavior of Charles II, as the licensers' rebuke ("luxury" instead of "lechery") and censorship verify. Moreover, Charles himself was not above finding amusement at theatrical depictions of himself as a virile master of women. The metanarrative possibilities of using hints of his known liaisons with female actors are worthy of speculation.[49] Plus, the awareness of an audience more fully conscious of the king's behavior and now positioned by the Restoration stage in closer proximity to the action to comment on these potential allusions made such commentary part of the entertainment that the new staging encouraged. Charles II was known to react harshly to political commentary but seems to have taken moral rebuke (if he even recognized it) as part of his enjoyment in the play. The point to be made here is not simply that Polwhele is making a critique of the monarch's behavior, but that she seems intriguingly confident in doing so. Whoever E. Polwhele might have been, she seems sufficiently secure in her social position to take such a risk and, more importantly, definitely aware of the possibilities in entertaining her audience through sly suggestions of this kind to which they would respond. To try to align her depiction of the Duchess with any one consistent female position, though not erroneous, is nonetheless to miss the theatrical possibilities that an adept playwright could exploit.

Who Was E. Polwhele? What Her Play Suggests

Milhous and Hume, the editors of Polwhele's later play *The Frolicks*, have suggested a candidate for its authorship and for *The Faithful Virgins*: one "Elizabeth" Polwhele, whose name has come down in the scholarship, but previously without any corroborative documentary evidence. From their search they note that the earliest mention of Polwhele's *Frolicks* is from an 1856 sale catalogue of manuscripts, and there the author's name is listed as "Polwhele (Elizabeth)," the parentheses apparently signifying conjecture. The manuscript in the Cornell University Library is titled in full, "THE FROLICKS; or the LAWYER CHEATED, a New Comedy, the first copy written by Mrs. E. P. 1671." Justification for the last name Polwhele is supplied by the signature "E. Polewheele" in the dedicatory letter

49. For a specific account of the king's liaisons, particularly with Lady Castlemaine, and later with Mary "Moll" Davis and Nell Gwyn, see Ronald Hutton, *Charles the Second: King of England, Scotland, and Ireland* (Oxford: Clarendon Press, 1989), 188–89, 262.

addressed to Prince Rupert attached to the Cornell manuscript. There is no similar documentation for the first name as Elizabeth.[50]

The candidate whom the Cornell editors, Milhous and Hume, propose is, as they state, "a rather startling one." She is "Elizabeth Polwhele," daughter of Theophilus Polwhele, a vicar of Tiverton, "a prominent nonconformist minister." His eldest daughter, Elizabeth Polwhele, married another nonconformist preacher, Stephen Lobb. Nothing else of this Elizabeth Polwhele has been discovered to date, nor is there any indication that she was even literate. As the Cornell editors admit, "One must grant that a virgin daughter from a very religious nonconformist family makes an odd candidate for so racy and au courant a play as *The Frolicks*"—or, for that matter, *The Faithful Virgins*, given its overtly licentious nature in many places throughout.[51]

One might discover a more fruitful avenue of research by looking more closely at what *The Faithful Virgins* and *The Frolicks*—and the dedicatory letter attached to the latter—of E. Polwhele tell us. More specifically, the kind of author the two plays and the letter suggest is someone quite different from the daughter and wife of nonconformist ministers. The dedicatory letter to Prince Rupert[52] is an important piece of documentary evidence and thus essential to quote here in full (see also Fig. 2).

> Present this humbly
> to the illustrious and
> most gracious Prince,
> Prince Rupert
>
> Mighty Prince,
>
> An unfortunate young woman begs she may not be more luckless in the presumption of her dedication of a thing of this nature to your Highness than all the others who are haunted with poetic devils like me—that so disquiet us we cannot find in our hearts to let our betters rest. Fame, great sir, has told me your grace is merciful to those that molest you with troubles of this nature. She farther adds you have a mind so bright and glorious that it does not only light us poor admiring mortals to adore you, but like the free and splendid eye of heaven, the sun, ye with a gentle influence look and shine on everything beneath you. Encouraged much by Mistress Fame I have for some minutes thrown my foolish modesty aside, and with

50. For discussion of the Cornell editors' search, and their findings of Theophilus Polwhele and Stephen Lobb, see Milhous and Hume, introduction to *The Frolicks*, 36–37, 44–49.

51. Milhous and Hume, introduction to *The Frolicks*, 44–45.

52. Prince Rupert (1619–1682) was the third son of Elizabeth Stuart, eldest daughter of James VI, and Frederick V of the Palatinate. For more on Prince Rupert, see p. 25.

> a boldness that does not well become a virgin, presume to offer this comedy [i.e., *The Frolicks*] at your Grace's feet, from whence you may spurn it into nothing, if in anything it can offend you. I dare not hope there is ingenuity enough in it to challenge much favor, but I must declare it is free from abusing any person. I question not but I shall be taxed for writing a play so comical, but those that have ever seen my *Faithful Virgins* and my *Elysium*[53] will justify me a little for writing this. I am young, no scholar, and what I write I write by nature, not by art. My careless stars so heedlessly do guide me as if they were unconcern'd with me, and my affairs lead me to nothing that is fortunate. But I shall grow incapable of misery, forget all their indifferent usage of me, and think that they oblige me above all I can ever merit from them, if on this hour they'll be so kind to smile, in which I implore your Highness' pardon for my unparallel'd boldness, as I am a woman, and your protection for this comedy, to whom I humbly dedicate and commit it, who am a true honorer of your Highness' virtues, and your most luckless but devoted servant,
>
> E. Polewheele[54]

The Cornell editors read this letter somewhat literally, again seeing Polwhele as a young, rather innocent and inexperienced writer, an interpretation that they then read back into her plays, particularly *The Faithful Virgins*.[55] Given the tradition of such dedications, however, with their rhetoric of decorous humility, one might instead read this letter as yet another instance of successful performance. That is, it is quite clear that in reading her letter in a performative context, one can conclude that Polwhele has skillfully mastered its tongue-in-cheek rhetoric. Shakespeare's dedicatory letters to the patrons of his narrative poems are the best known of such performances.[56] Thus, reading such documents literally requires some measure of caution. Instead, given the performative skill demonstrated in this letter, and the apparent awareness of the technicalities of the new stage as demonstrated by both of her plays, one might better search for E. Polwhele from a different direction, from among those with experience in the Restoration court.

53. The *Elysium* is no longer extant but may have been a masque.

54. E. Polwhele, *The Frolicks; or, The Lawyer Cheated (1671)*, ed. Judith Milhous and Robert D. Hume (Ithaca, NY: Cornell University Press, 1977), 57–58.

55. Milhous and Hume, introduction to *The Frolicks*, 41–43.

56. See his "Venus and Adonis," the dedication to Southampton, for example, which begins, "I know not how I shall offend in dedicating my unpolished lines to your lordship," and continues in the language of appropriately decorous humility. His dedicatory letter appended to "The Rape of Lucrece" is similarly described as "my untutored lines" and adds, "were my worth greater my duty would show greater."

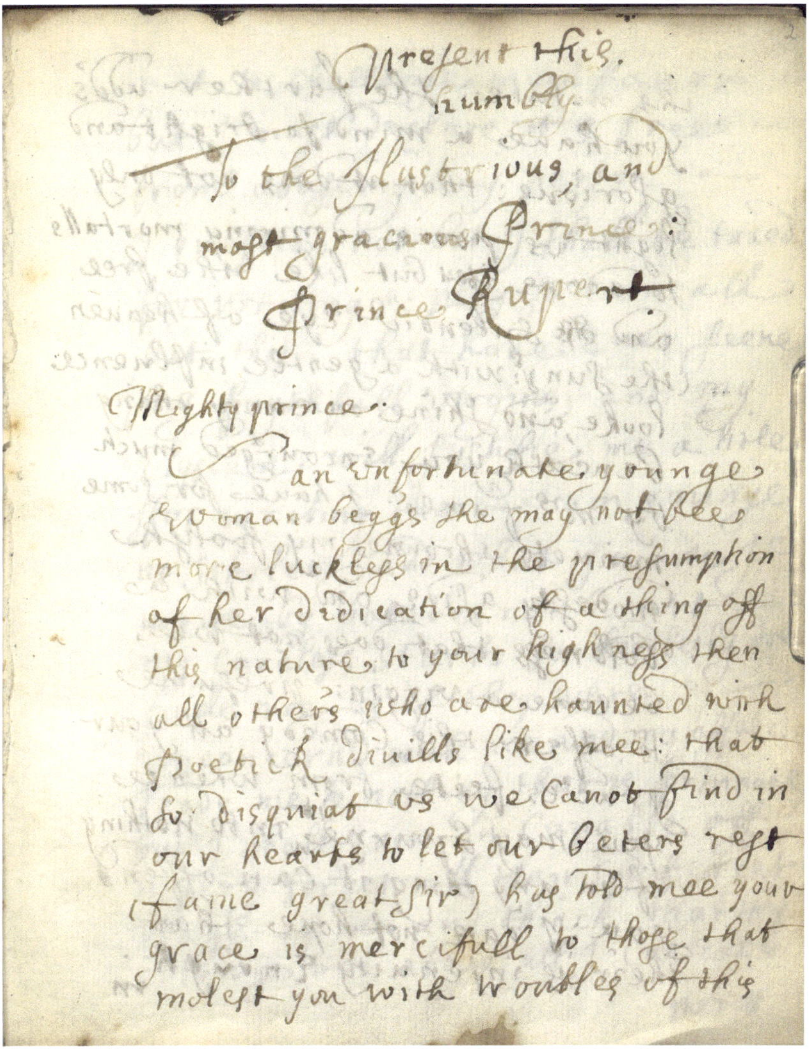

Present this
humbly
To the Illustrious, and
most gracious Prince:
Prince Rupert.

Mighty prince.
an unfortunate younge
woman beggs she may not bee
more luckless in the presumption
of her dedication of a thing off
this nature, to your highness then
all others who are haunted with
poetick divills like mee: that
so disquiat us we canot find in
our hearts to let our betters rest
(fame great Sir) has told mee your
grace is mercifull to those that
molest you with troubles of this

Figure 2. Letter of dedication to Prince Rupert, *The Frolicks*. Cornell University Library, Ithaca, NY. Archives 4600 Bd. MS 143 (formerly MSS Bd. Rare P P77), leaf 2r.

Like *The Faithful Virgins*, Polwhele's second extant play, *The Frolicks*, demonstrates a similar court and theatrical awareness. Its format, a series of rapidly shifting scenes, would again seem to have been designed for the new scenic theater. Moreover, this second play, a comedy, demonstrates a sophisticated awareness of audience both in its potential for casting with an eye to the behaviors of Charles II and his court, and in its shift to what would become the comedy of manners in the next decade. Its cast includes not only a witty couple but also a deft awareness of female roles. Most notably, it is strikingly aware of the constriction of women in its use of cross-dressing, where instead of women in male clothing, male characters are trapped in female attire and then denied (by the playwright) an opportunity to change out of that clothing.[57]

Given the sophistication of the background implied by both plays and the dedicatory letter, then, searching for E. Polwhele might be more efficacious if one begins with that background rather than from assumptions about "Elizabeth" as Polwhele's first name. A woman whose name begins with *E*, yet who comes from a social class associated with courtly behaviors and particularly its theatrical interests, might better fit the profile implied by the two plays and the letter. It is by no means definitive, but such an individual may well have existed. That possibility is one Elnora Polwhele, who may have been part of the Fitton–Leveson branch of the Newdigates of the seventeenth-century gentry, which included, from Shakespeare's era, one Mary Fitton, lady-in-waiting in Elizabeth's court, who married "William Polewheele of Perton, d. 1610."[58] While Vivienne Larminie's Newdigate genealogy chart leaves off with the Fitton marriage and the record of a son, "William Polewheele," an "Elnora Polewheele" was recorded at the same time as the daughter of "Guilliemus [William] Polewheele," married to "Jana," with a date of christening (September 21, 1643) that would fit well with the age of a playwright of the 1660s.[59] Although both the date of christening and the correspondence of paternal name fit well with an "Elnora" as the same person as the daughter of the Newdigate relative, William Polwhele, there is as yet no definitive evidence connecting the two. The coincidence, however, is definitely tempting to investigate further.

The daughters of the Newdigate family, and its Fitton–Leveson branch, would have had the education, theatrical associations, and court connections to have produced both the plays and the skillfully composed dedicatory letter written by E. Polwhele. Larminie describes the Newdigate women at length as being, in general, articulate and persuasive women who could move skillfully in a world apparently dominated by men. The conventions of modesty and politeness apart, they were not inhibited in applying to the opposite sex for help or patronage. They were literate, could write well, and were occasionally complimented on their

57. See discussions of *The Frolicks* in the context of female social roles in several essays including, in particular, Findlay, "Licensed to Thrill." The scene in Polwhele's *Frolicks* closes without allowing the male characters to change back into male attire, something they comment on, thus specifically calling attention to the playwright's influence in closing the scene while leaving them so trapped.

58. The aristocratic and educated background of the Newdigate women is traced in detail in Vivienne M. Larminie, *Wealth, Kinship, and Culture: The Seventeenth-Century Newdigates of Arbury and Their World* (Woodbridge, Suffolk: Boydell Press, 1995). The genealogical chart relevant to the Mary Fitton line of this family can be found on p. 212.

59. Elnora Polewheele, "Baptismal Record," Staffordshire Record Office, D1364/1/1. St. Michael and All Angels, Tettenhall Regis, Parish Register, 1643.

handwriting.[60] All of these descriptions are equally applicable to the female playwright who composed Polwhele's plays and wrote the dedicatory letter.

That letter, as we have seen, is addressed to Prince Rupert, a close relative of the royal family, a leading military figure, and, most importantly, a dedicated patron and supporter of the new theaters. He was a friend of the manager of the King's Men, Thomas Killigrew, who had dedicated one of his plays to him, and his mistress was the actress Margaret Hughes. Not only was he thus an excellent theatrical choice as dedicatee of Polwhele's *Frolicks*, but he was also someone of significant social and political importance. A young, unknown, provincial figure would have hardly dared to approach him much less make a public appeal for his support. That Prince Rupert might have actually attended a performance of Polwhele's earliest extant play, *The Faithful Virgins*, is also implied by the wording of this dedication, in which she remarks that those who have "seen" that earlier play would "justify" her new drama. The emphasis on "seen" may thus imply attendance at a performance of *The Faithful Virgins*, and not simply that its script had been read.

Moreover, Margaret Hughes as Prince Rupert's mistress is particularly pertinent in establishing a context of court connections for the writer of *The Faithful Virgins* and *The Frolics*, as the autograph signature, "Arthur Hewes 1681," appears on leaf 4r of the manuscript of the later play. Evidently, the manuscript of this play was owned by someone in the Hughes family, and it remained in their possession for at least a decade. The relationship between Margaret Hughes and Arthur Hewes/Hughes is not known, but the familial connection strengthens the implication that the author of these plays had connections in court circles of some note.

An additional piece of evidence for E. Polwhele as someone other than the daughter of a nonconformist minister appears in a broadside ballad printed in 1672 and attributed to "Mrs. E. P." in praise of James, Duke of York, Lord High Admiral (and later king after the death of his brother, Charles II).[61] Its opening line—"Proud Hogen, Mogen's, we will make you bow"—taunts the Dutch (the "High and Mighty") by alluding to the Dutch States General and praises "brave *York*." The comments throughout its satiric content reveal a detailed level of commercial and political awareness consistent with a writer knowledgeable about court commentary and political affairs. If "Mrs. E. P." is the same "E. P." of the

60. Larminie, *Wealth*, 88–90 and *passim*.

61. See Fig. 8 in the Appendix. The poem, "On His Royal Highness: His Expedition against the Dutch," is transcribed and "tentatively attributed" to Elizabeth Polwhele by Jane Stevenson and Peter Davidson, who cite it as P 19B from the second edition of Wing's *Short-Title Catalogue*; see Elizabeth Polwhele, "On His Royal Highness: His Expedition against the Dutch," in *Early Modern Women Poets: An Anthology*, ed. Jane Stevenson and Peter Davidson (Oxford: Oxford University Press, 2006), 408–11. As Stevenson and Davidson suggest, "The royalism of this ballad would be compatible with [Polwhele's] dedication of *The Frolics* to Prince Rupert, and also renders an Anglican background more probable than a Non-conformist one" (409). They also suggest that Elizabeth Polwhele's father might have been John Polwhele (1586–1614), a fellow of Exeter College at Oxford and later vicar of Whitechurch in Devon.

letter to Prince Rupert and two timely plays, this poem too suggests a writer of both wit and court connections.

Finally, returning us to the name Elizabeth, a trace of an "Elizabeth Polwhele" is located in a signature on the title page of a book, *The Gentlewomans Companion; or, A Guide to the Female Sex*, by Hannah Woolley, found in the British Library (BL C.194.a1455).[62] The signature reads, "Elizabeth Polwheile Her Booke." The handwriting, while not exactly the same as the handwriting of Polwhele's two play manuscripts, is close enough to be noteworthy, and the topic of the book is certainly consistent with the female focus of Polwhele's two extant plays.

While the editors of *The Frolicks*, Milhous and Hume, were somewhat dismissive of Polwhele's earlier play, *The Faithful Virgins*, they conclude their discussion of her as a playwright with a strong endorsement of her dramatic skill: "Whoever 'E. Polewheele' may have been, we have at the very least to grant that she wrote two quite professional plays at a date when female playwriting was almost unknown. . . . On the basis of her two efforts extant, she must be accounted an impressively observant and ambitious pioneer."[63] To this endorsement we can add that while a playwright composes her plays, in Polwhele's case, her plays, with their astute use of staging, awareness of audience, and significant courtly context of social connections and allusions, can also be said to compose her, an intriguing playwright, and one worthy of further reading and study.

The Manuscript of The Faithful Virgins

The only known manuscript copy of Polwhele's *The Faithful Virgins* is located in the archives of the Bodleian Library at Oxford University bound in a larger manuscript collection, MS. Rawl. poet. 195, on folio leaves 49–78, along with five other manuscripts. Included among these is the posthumous play by Aphra Behn, *The Younger Brother*.[64] All are on paper in different handwriting described by the Bodleian *Summary Catalogue* as "17th cent."[65] The binding of the larger manuscript is pasteboard covered with the remains of a parchment document, typical

62. See Fig. 7 in the Appendix. The signature was found by the British Library and posted on their Twitter account, @BLprintheritage. I am grateful to Martine van Elk for calling my attention to this.

63. Milhous and Hume, introduction to *The Frolicks*, 49.

64. The full title of this work as it appears in the Oxford manuscript is "The Younger Brother, or the amorous jilt, a comedy . . . by the late ingenious Mrs. Behn," which is preceded by an account of the author.

65. Falconer Madan, ed., A *Summary Catalogue of Western Manuscripts in the Bodleian Library at Oxford*, Vol. 3, *Collections Received During the 18th Century* (Oxford: Clarendon Press, 1895), no. 14687. The other manuscripts, in addition to Aphra Behn's, are the plays "Susenbrotus, comoedia. Acta Cantabrigiae in collegio Trin. coram rege Jacobo & Carolo principe, anno 1615"; "Iugurtha, or the fait[h]less cosen German, a tragedy"; and "The Sixth Satyr of Juvenall made English"; and a set of poems entitled "Sweden's Lamentation," "Epistle to Zaretta," and "The Batchelor."

of the cheap bindings usually made for Richard Rawlinson, as the Bodleian's *Summary Catalogue* also notes. All of the smaller manuscripts within this larger one, including the manuscript of *The Faithful Virgins*, are unbound, on paper.

Richard Rawlinson (1689/90–1755) was a collector of books, manuscripts, and other rarities. He bequeathed most of his collection to the Bodleian in his will of 1756, but nothing is known of when or from where he collected most of the items, including the manuscripts of these plays. On the front cover of MS. Rawl. poet. 195 are some faint notations that may indicate the transfer of the larger manuscript, perhaps from a binder, from a "Sir Thomas Selright" to a "Dr. Thelwell Dean" on "Dec. 19, 1726." Other names faintly discernable are "Mr. William Thomas of London," "Mr. Combey," "Mr. Tottenham of Linc [*sic*]," "Mr. Torkington, Rector of Shottefroke," and "Dr. Thorpe of Rochester." These individuals may have nothing to do with the manuscript, the names being, perhaps, simply notes for some other transaction if the paper for the binding had been repurposed. On the back cover of MS. Rawl. poet. 195 there is, however, the notation, "For Dr. Rawlinson," scrawled faintly across some illegible writing with the year "1746." Beyond these faint clues, if they are such, there is nothing known of the provenance the manuscript.

The *Summary Catalogue* also notes that the six manuscripts in MS. Rawl. poet. 195 are "in different formats and at different times and that there is no obvious connection among them apart from the fact that most of them are plays."[66] Close inspection of the handwriting of Polwhele's manuscript, however, does suggest some possibly useful data. A largely italic script with no idiosyncratic features, it is very similar to the handwriting of the manuscript for Polwhele's comedy *The Frolicks* (see Fig. 3). Moreover, it is also evidently the same handwriting used for the dedicatory letter of that same play (Fig. 2). What is particularly interesting, however, is the handwriting on the last page of the manuscript for *The Faithful Virgins*. The verso side of this page had evidently been used at one time as a scratch sheet—perhaps repurposed for the last page of the play as the writing is upside down from the body of the play, the last page of which is on the recto side. It includes part of what is possibly an alchemical recipe mixing "golde" and "mercury" followed by two incomplete sentences in handwriting that seems very different from that of the play: "My Lord pray remember me, when you . . ." and "My Lord pray think on me when you doe [illegible] . . ." Finally, in the middle of the same page, in slightly different handwriting again, is the fervent, "Lord Jesus rescue my soul Amen," signed, with a flourish, by the initials "E.[K?]." The Cornell editors read these initials as "E. P.," and while the two capital *E*s are similar, the second letter is not as clearly a *P*. Thus, it seems unlikely, given the different handwriting, that most of these final jottings were written in the hand that wrote the plays. Nonetheless, binding, paper, some handwriting, notations not connected directly with the play—all of these are tantalizing clues as to provenance

66. Madan, *Summary Catalogue*.

and authorship. Finally, did Polwhele use a scribe for her two plays? This seems unlikely as the dedicatory letter shares a similar handwriting. Thus, one might fairly conclude that the writing of both plays and letter, as evidenced by handwriting, was done by the same person, at least possibly Polwhele herself.

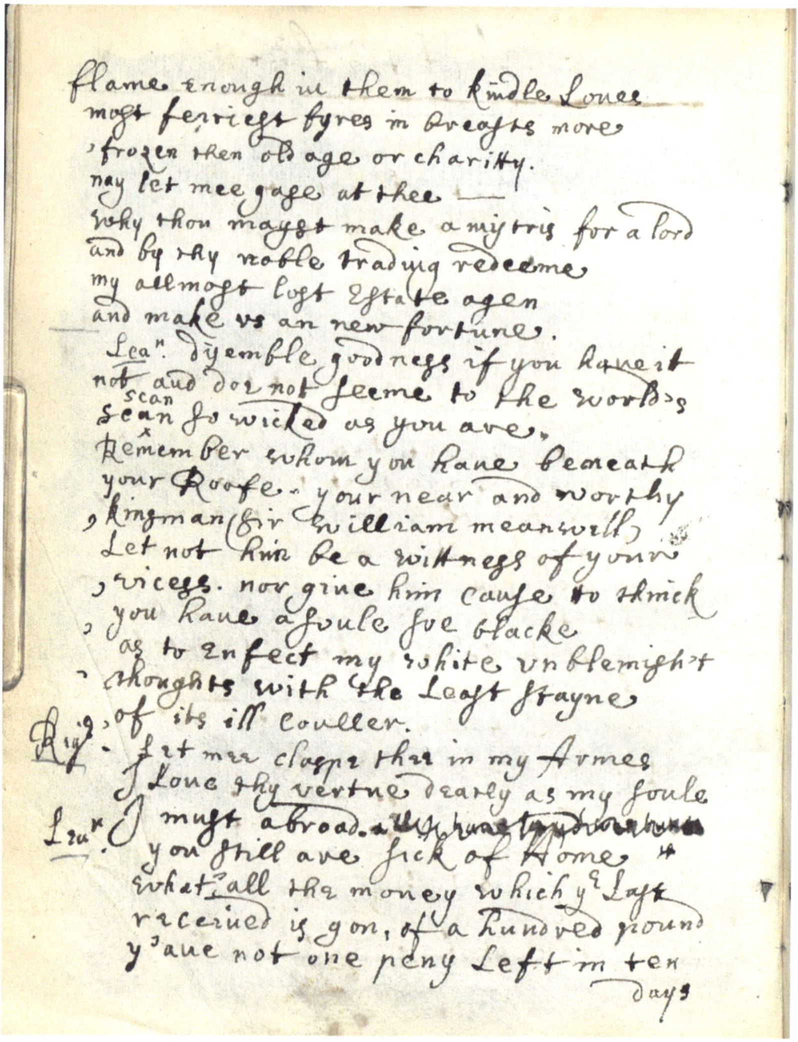
flame enough in them to kindle Loves
most fervent fyres in breasts more
frozen then old age or charity.
nay let mee gaze at thee —
why thou mayst make a mistris for a Lord
and by thy noble trading redeeme
my allmost lost Estate agen
and make vs an new fortune.
Lea[n]. dissemble goodness if you have it
not and doe not seeme to the worlds
scan so wicked as you are.
Remember whom you have beneath
your Roofe. your near and worthy
kinsman (Sir William meanwell)
Let not him be a witness of your
vices. nor give him cause to think
you have a soule soe blacke
as to infect my white vnblemish't
thoughts with the Least stayne
of its ill couller.
Rig. Let mee claspe thee in my Armes
I love thy vertue dearly as my soule
Lea. I must abroad. [illegible]
you still are sick of Home
what all the money which y[e] Last
receiued is gon, of a hundred pound
y'aue not one peny Left in ten
days

Figure 3. Manuscript page from Polwhele's later play, *The Frolicks*. Cornell University Library, Ithaca, NY. Archives 4600 Bd. MS 143 (formerly MSS Bd. Rare P P77), leaf 5v.

One last detail to be considered is the paper and binding of the two plays. While the paper for *The Frolicks* seems to have been more carefully chosen and possibly more expensive, the paper on which *The Faithful Virgins* is recorded is cheap,[67] the manuscript consisting of thirty leaves of a lesser quality British laid paper, all of the same character, size, and dull cream color. The leaves measure 283 x 182 mm and have seven chain lines 23 mm apart; fourteen of the thirty leaves contain a fleur-de-lis watermark very similar to one noted in Edward Heawood's *Watermarks*.[68]

Similarly, unlike the pasteboard cover typical of the cheap bindings of the larger Rawlinson manuscript, the binding of Polwhele's *Frolicks* is an attractive red leather "similar to that produced by the Court binder for Charles II."[69] The contrast between bindings implies that the manuscript for the later play was contemporaneous with Polwhele herself, while the manuscript for the earlier play was bound with five others by Rawlinson in the early eighteenth century. One could conclude that the purpose of the manuscript for *The Faithful Virgins*, with its attached license from theatrical authorities, was professional, at least in its implication of performance, while the manuscript for the second play was intended to be read by someone who would find its binding and dedicatory letter appropriate for aristocratic readers. Most importantly, then, the implication of both manuscripts is that E. Polwhele had theatrical support as well as education and social position reflective of court connections. Thus, whatever "E." Polwhele's first name might have been, and whoever she actually was, those circles seem to be where she and her plays belong.

Note on the Text

As noted earlier, the only known extant manuscript of *The Faithful Virgins* is located in the archives of the Bodleian Library at Oxford University in MS Rawl. poet. 195, fols. 49–78. It is quite legible. The handwriting, spelling, and punctuation are very similar to that of the manuscript of her other later play, *The Frolicks* (1671), published by Cornell University Press in 1977. Like the Cornell editors, and following practices used in other editions in The Other Voice series, I have modernized my transcription of Polwhele's work to conform to modern American practices with regard to both spelling and punctuation, but have retained those instances where meaning is clear to convey original style and intention. I have added line numbers in units of five for the convenience of readers.

67. Milhous and Hume identify it as consisting of three kinds of paper: two lightweight papers alternating apparently at random, and a Spanish paper used for the outer, blank leaves and title page.

68. Edward Heawood, ed., *Watermarks, Mainly of the 17th and 18th Centuries* (Hilversum, Holland: Paper Publications Society, 1950), pl. 1718.

69. Milhous and Hume, introduction to *The Frolicks*, 33.

Because *The Faithful Virgins* is written in rhymed couplets, I have had to alter the capitalization of the manuscript considerably, most specifically in capitalizing the first letter in each line. As Polwhele's capitalization in other places is rather irregular, I have modernized those instances as well. I have retained contractions to preserve meter where important, and I have expanded abbreviations and other contractions where necessary. I have regularized the letters *u*/*v*, *i*/*j*, and the long *s*. I have also added a descriptive list of characters preceding the play since a *dramatis personae* is not included in the manuscript.

Where the manuscript abbreviates names of characters, I have spelled these out in full and in capital letters with the exception of the character of Floradine. The manuscript consistently presents her name in lowercase letters, perhaps to signify that this character, who enters as a male page, is in fact a woman disguised for the usual reason that she is in love with the lord she serves, Statenor, but cannot declare her love, a familiar plot device. I have thus retained the lowercase signification for "floradine" as a distinctive feature of the text. I have also retained the "X" marks made by Henry Herbert in the margins of the original manuscript as an additional distinctive feature, thus informing the modern reader of these significant elements in the original that would have been otherwise lost in transcription.

The manuscript is clearly divided into acts but not into scenes. I have not inserted scene divisions as that seems counter to the usual practice in Restoration manuscripts, but I have, instead, inserted footnotes where scene changes are important, particularly in regard to location.

THE FAITHFUL VIRGINS

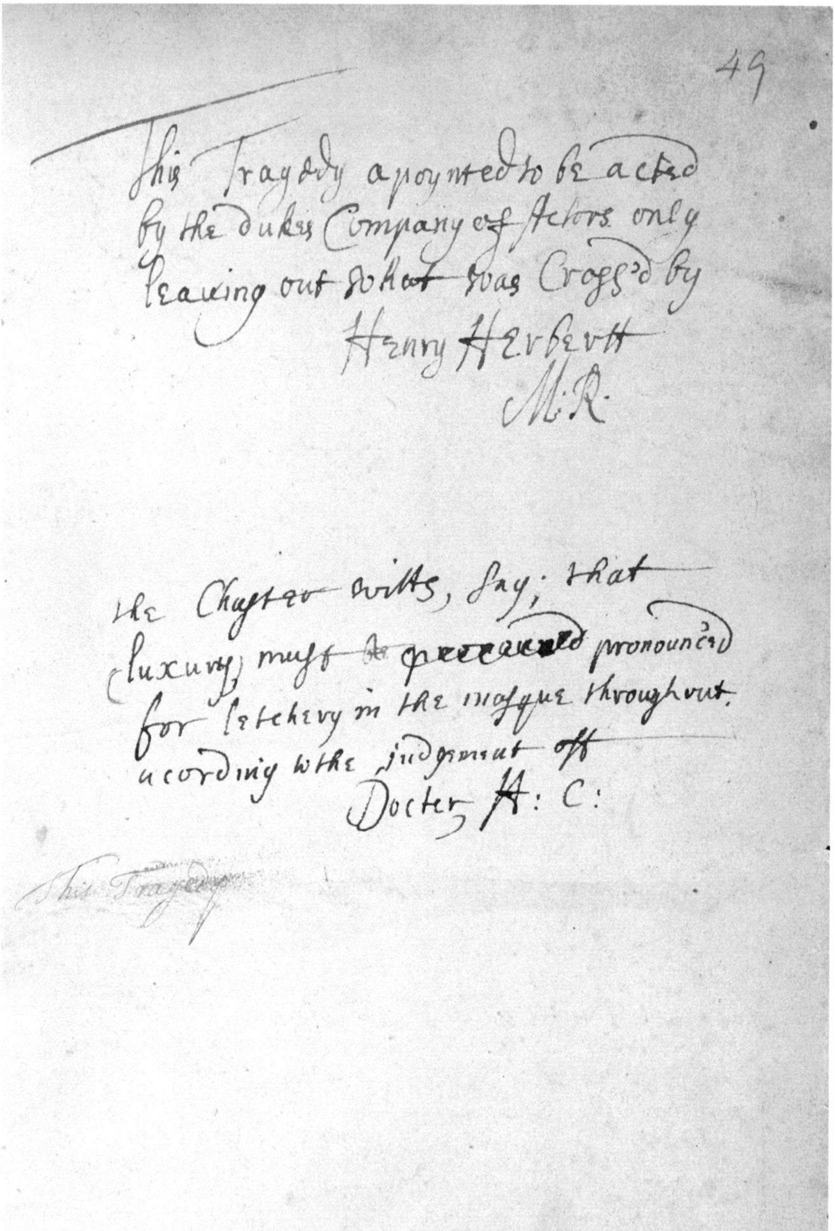
This Tragedy apoynted to be acted
by the dukes Company of Actors only
leaving out what was Cross'd by
Henry Herbert
M:R:

the Chapter witts, say; that
luxury, must be pronounced
for letchery in the masque throughout
according to the judgment of
Docter H: C:

Figure 4. First page of *The Faithful Virgins*. Bodleian Library, Oxford. MS. Rawl. poet. 195, fol. 49r.

This tragedy appointed to be acted
by the Duke's Company of Actors[1] only
leaving out what was crossed[2] by
Henry Herbert
M. R.[3]

The Chaster[4] Wits say that
"luxury" must be pronounced
for "lechery" in the masque[5] throughout,
according with the judgment of
Doctor H. C.[6]

PERSONS[7]

Men

The Duke. Of Tuscany. He has been courting Isabella and marries her midway through the play but then falls in love with Umira, one of the faithful virgins, and abandons his duchess.

Philammon. A young lord. Dead when the play begins. The faithful virgins gather around his tomb and lament his death, remaining "faithful" to him throughout the play.

Statenor. A young lord. Brother of Umira. Falls in love with Merantha and courts her throughout the play, but is loved by Erasila, in disguise as his page, Floradine.

1. The Duke's Company, managed by Sir William Davenant (1660–1668) and performing at Lincoln's Inn Fields Theater. See Introduction, pp. 6–8.

2. "Crossed" indicates that the use of a particular passage is prohibited; the crosses are drawn into the margins of this text.

3. See Richard Dutton, "Herbert, Sir Henry (*bap.* 1594, *d.* 1673)," in *ODNB*, ed. Lawrence Dutton (Oxford: Oxford University Press, 2004), https://doi.org/10.1093/ref:odnb/13029. "M. R." indicates "Master of the Revels," the title for the official in charge of censoring and licensing plays, a position that Herbert held from 1623 to 1673. See Introduction, p. 7. While we have no record of actual performance, the copy of Herbert's notation of license almost certainly certifies that *The Faithful Virgins* was performed, most likely by Davenant's company as noted here.

4. "Chaster" apparently refers to the censoring role played by the Master of the Revels; there is no such variation recorded in the *OED*.

5. Of the masque in act 3, where Lechery appears as a character, see Introduction, p. 20. The censurers prefer a reference to the Latin *luxuria*, or Luxury.

6. Doctor H. C. has not been identified; he may have been one of the assistants to the Master of the Revels.

7. The list of characters and their descriptions has been supplied by the editor. See "Note on the Text," Introduction, p. 30.

CLEOPHON. Another young lord. Brother of Merantha. Loves Isabella but has lost her to the Duke. Becomes the new Duke of Tuscany at the end of the play.

TRASILIUS. Another young lord. Hired by Isabella to assassinate the Duke.

FRANCISCUS. Another young lord. Confidant of Trasilius.

EUMENUS and CLEON. Two older lords. Supporters of the Duchess.

Women

THE DUCHESS. Isabella. Once betrothed to Cleophon but gives him up to marry the Duke.

MERANTHA. One of the faithful virgins. Loved Philammon and remains by his hearse to lament his death, thus "faithful" to him throughout the play. Sister of Cleophon. Rejects Statenor.

UMIRA. The other faithful virgin, also loved Philammon; remains with Merantha at his hearse to lament his death and be equally "faithful." Rejects the Duke. Sister to Statenor.

ERASILA. Actually disguised as the page, Floradine, to follow Statenor, whom she loves. Sister to Philammon. In the manuscript, she is consistently listed as "floradine."

Minor characters

Masquers, representing a variety of sins—Detraction, Envy, Ambition, Lechery, Pride, Flattery, Avarice, Drunkenness (with five dancing "drunks")—and seven virtues—Chastity, Virtue, Humility, Patience, Justice, Prudence, and Sobriety.

Three witches.

Several Gentlemen, Pages, and one Angel.

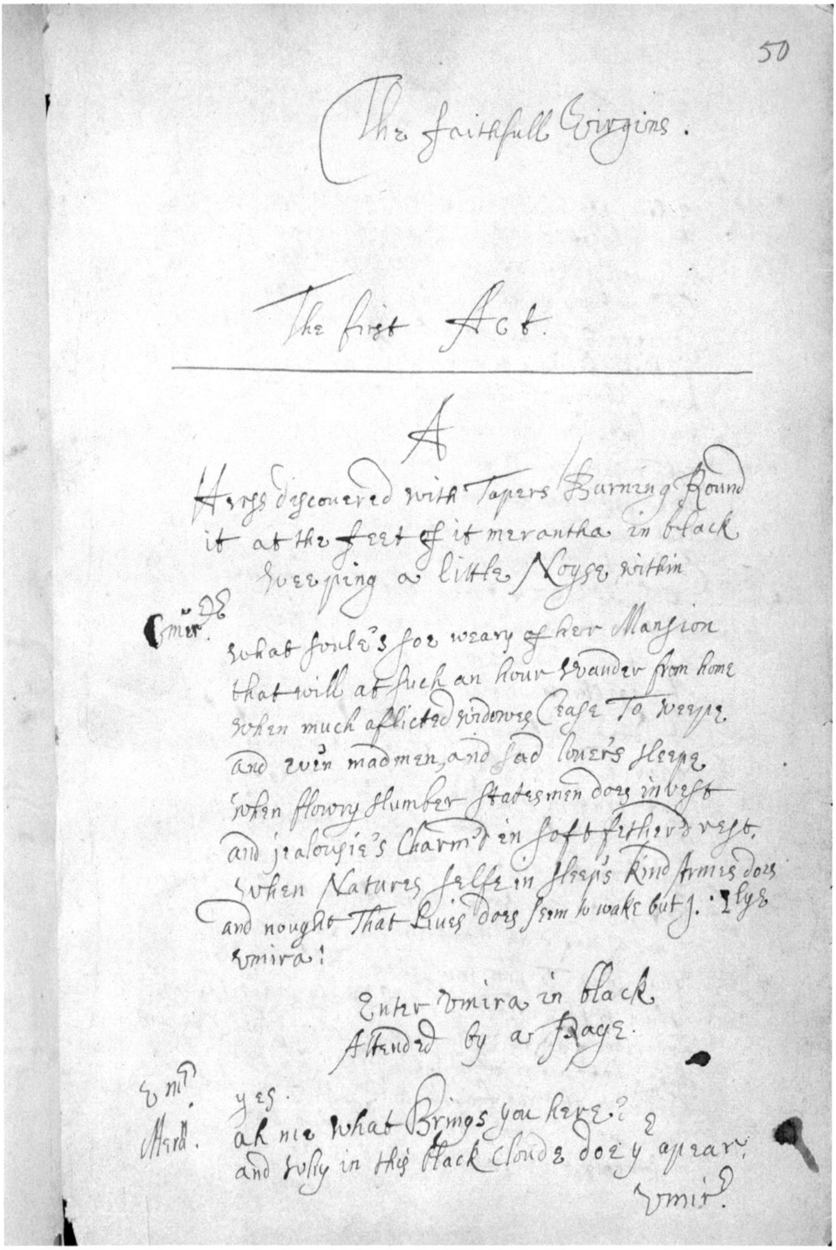

Figure 5. First page of the text of *The Faithful Virgins*. Bodleian Library, Oxford. MS. Rawl. poet. 195, fol. 50r.

The Faithful Virgins

The First Act

A hearse discovered[8] with tapers burning round it. At the feet of it, MERANTHA in black, weeping. A little noise [from] within.

MERANTHA. What soul's so weary of her mansion
That will at such an hour wander from home,
When much afflicted widows cease to weep,
And even madmen and sad lovers sleep;
When flowry slumber statesmen does invest
And Jealousy's charms in soft feathers rest;
When Nature's self in Sleep's kind arms does lie,
And naught that lives does seem to wake but I.
Umira!

Enter UMIRA in black, attended by a PAGE.

UMIRA. Yes.

MERANTHA. Ah me. What brings you here?
And why in this black cloud do you appear?

UMIRA. Where the affections of a heart do lie,
The soul at liberty will thither fly.
I, much submitted to a brother's sway,
Could not my duty to these ashes pay
Sooner, but have been forced to suffer thee,
In that obedience to outrival me.
Know, though Philammon did to you pretend,[9]
Your love for him could not my flame transcend.

MERANTHA. Why, Madame, would you whilst he was conceal
That passion you so freely now reveal,[10]
That our Philammon might have paid to you
What to your eyes and to your flame was due.

UMIRA. I loved not to enjoy, but with desires
That were extracted from Love's noblest fires.

8. "Made manifest; found out, revealed" (*OED*, s.v. "discovered"). An indication that the stage shutters have been opened to expose an action in progress. For discovery scenes, see Introduction, pp. 8–9.

9. Used here in its seventeenth-century sense of "offer" rather than "dissemble" (*OED*, s.v. "pretend").

10. That is, while he was alive.

Virtue could not my passion disapprove,
For as chaste virgins worthy brothers love,
I loved Philammon, though I knew that he,
Dear maid, had offered his soul's vows to thee.
But that in me no envy did create,
For I did love him at no common rate.
And from his urn I never will remove,
But stay and weep with thee o're what we love.

MERANTHA. I am amazed at that which you design.
Your love to him, my glory will outshine.

UMIRA. Thine to the world hath first its higher shown,
And from fame's voice hath purchased such renown
That what I do will but appear to be
A shadow of that faith which shines in thee.

MERANTHA. Since you so nobly have resolved to be
In sorrow Competitress[11] with me,
Here let us faithfully divide our grief,
'Till death to love and sorrow gives relief.

UMIRA. What way of grief that which you pursue,
Tell me, that I at least may grieve like you.

MERANTHA. Though faithful virgins, Madame, may be taught
By me to grieve such losses as they ought,
I'll not presume to teach you what to do,
But strive in grief to sympathize with you.

UMIRA. In grief we'll rivals be, and let her boast
How well she loved, Merantha, that grieves most.

The hearse is shut in.[12]

STATENOR enters at one door; at another, floradine.[13]

STATENOR. Welcome my sweetest floradine, what news?

11. Perhaps a feminine form of "competitor." Merantha goes on to suggest that they mourn Philammon together rather than be at odds with one another.

12. A stage direction: the shutters are to be closed so that neither the hearse nor its mourners can be seen on stage.

13. Floradine's name is written in lowercase letters throughout the manuscript, perhaps to indicate that she is a woman in male disguise. In this role, the actress's performance would thus accentuate the "breeches part," in which the female leg encased in male attire (breeches) is seductively on display.

FLORADINE. Umira's page, Sir, for the honor sues
To speak with you. Something he would impart.

STATENOR. Admit him.

Enter PAGE in mourning.

Ha! In black. Fear strikes my heart
With a chill cold, sharp as the hand of death,
Or frosts, that kill the flowers in their birth.
Where is Umira? Tell me. With the dead—
Is her bless'd spirit from its mansion fled
That thou these black and such sad looks doest wear.
Speak, and the fatal truth to me declare.

PAGE. My lady lives.

STATENOR. Ha, prithee, speak't again.

PAGE. She lives, and yet does with the dead remain.

STATENOR. Unriddle, for thy words mysterious are.
Give me the meaning of them in my ear.

They whisper aside.

Umira? Love Philammon?

PAGE. Yes, Sir, beyond
All passions, Sir, that love can comprehend.
There with the faithful virgin she will live,
And as they equally did love, they grieve
By turns, my lord, o're him so loved, they mourn
And pay their sighs and tears at his cold urn.
Whilst famed Merantha wakes, Umira sleeps,
And like a chaste and watchful vestal[14] keeps
Alive that flame love kindled in her breast,
Where it can ne'r be quenched, nor once suppressed.

STATENOR. Such flames grow sick of time and quickly die.
And time in them will kill that vanity.
Love in our breasts can hold but little room,
When the effect that made us love is gone.
Conduct me where Philammon's body's laid.
I mean from thence my sister to persuade.

14. "Chaste" or "pure"; usually associated with the Vestal Virgins, Roman priestesses who cultivated a sacred fire that was never allowed to go out.

Exeunt omnes.[15]

Enter CLEOPHON, sadly.

CLEOPHON. Ye gods, why did you Beauty e're create?
If you could mean man should be fortunate . . .

Enter ISABELLA, like a bride, attended by the bridal ladies.

CLEOPHON. Ha! Thus the world's great light at his uprise
Displays his glory to our wondering eyes.
Good heavens, what is he! That would once believe
That falsehood in so bright a form could live.
But I, who by experience know that faith
In this admired shape no being hath.
Those charming looks revive my dying flame
And should ensnare my soul to death again,
Were it not fortified against surprise.
I must no more be ruined by those eyes.

[He] offers to go.[16]

Though I move forward, yet my soul looks back
As though she were unwilling to forsake
That taking object, but she must not stay.
Love once in me shall reason's power obey.

He offers to go again.

ISABELLA. Shame will not suffer me to speak to him.
Why should frail mortals seem to blush at sin,
And dare to act it. I will speak though I,
Aurora-like,[17] in my own blushing die.
At my request, Sir, one short moment stay.
I've somewhat in my own defense to say,
Which you should hear—

CLEOPHON. How, in your own defense?
What can you say? Did ever innocence

15. Latin for "exit all."

16. Cleophon steps away, as if agreeing to leave if Isabella so wishes.

17. Like Aurora, the Roman goddess of the dawn.

Appear more lovely in unblemisht youth,
Why heaven such beauty made you without truth?

ISABELLA. Will you to my discourse vouchsafe an ear?

CLEOPHON. What can you treat of but how false you are
Unto the lost and wretched Cleophon,
And how much by your falsehood he's undone.
How he did more than his religion prize
The luster of Isabella, of those eyes,
Which crime deserved so strict a punishment,
That my loved sins become the instrument.
More, how their lights did only shine to me,
And bless'd no other with their lucencie.
If you and virtue but consistent were,
I needed not the cruel truth declare
That you from me have now withdrawn their light,
Like day that flies to other worlds from night.
Of this discourse I can no more admit,
For I grow desperate at the sense of it.

She weeps.

Why should you weep, and at ills you might redress,
If you were just, and so much grief express?
If it be not dissembled, you may yet
From the Duke's bosom make a safe retreat,
And shelter in these willing arms of mine,
Which shall protect you from the world and him.
And their protection cannot be denied,
Since you are not by ceremony tied.
I having yet more right to you than he.

ISABELLA. I'm promised him.[18]

CLEOPHON. But you were vowed to me.
Oh woman! Ever created to deceive.
Thy tears had almost fooled me to believe
That they were real, but 'twas in vain in me
To think that ought but falsehood dwelt in thee.
S:rH: Herbert X Go shackle with the Duke and be admired,[19]

18. I'm promised to him.

19. For the crosses in the margin before lines 137 and 141, see Fig. 6 and Introduction, p. 20. Perhaps Herbert thought these lines could be taken to refer to the king, Charles II, and thus might be potentially offensive.

'Till he is with some new sprung beauty fired,
Which will be swiftly, Isabella. He
Should have been woman for inconstancy.
S:rH: Herbert X He might have mistresses and often change,
And when he does, you must not think it strange.
Such shall the soul of Tuscany command,
Whilst a scorned wife must as a cypher stand.
Too soon you will the plague of greatness know,
When you shall be a princess scarce in show,
And much too late, fair Excellence, you'll seem
To wish you had more just and faithful been.

Exit CLEOPHON.

ISABELLA. Oh! What was that which Cleophon just said
That in my breast hath such impression made.

She swoons; the ladies support her.

Flourish.[20]

Enter EUMENUS, TRASILIUS, CLEON, *stare*[21] before the DUKE who is followed by COURTIERS, PAGES, and ATTENDANTS.

DUKE. Ha! Isabella.

EUMENUS. Oh, my child's dead.
Must a sad tomb become thy bridal bed?

CLEON. She lives, my lord.

DUKE. Her eyes their wonted light
Again resume, and charm my ravished sight.
The Persians thus behold their rising sun,
To which they sacrifice when night is gone.
Help, help! Their light is again o're cast,
As if such glory were too great to last.
The gods are envious, and sure fear that I
Should her possess they would themselves enjoy.
Her eyes again my fainting soul revive,
And flatter me to hope that I shall live.

20. Indicating a dramatic announcement, usually by trumpet.

21. Latin for "stand."

Speak, my beloved, and the sad cause impart
That hath sent such disorder to thy heart.

ISABELLA. An inward grief did my sick soul oppress,
Which did afflict me, Sir, even to excess.
But now 'tis vanished, and I'm healthy grown,
As if I had no such distemper known.

DUKE. Breathe to my soul once more this harmony,
Least I with fear I am deceived may die.

ISABELLA. I'm well my lord, so well I scarce retain
In memory that I felt any pain.
Sure that which Cleophon declared to me,
His malice rather than a truth should be.
(Aside) That tenderness the Duke has now expressed
Dispels all clouds of trouble in my breast.

DUKE. If this be no new mockery of fate,
To make me once again unfortunate,
By losing what I covet to possess,
Beyond all joys that men call happiness,
Come, let us to the temple, and there tie
And link our souls, or else together die.

Exeunt omnes.

Enter floradine, pensive.

floradine. Harsh god, why shouldst thou at my bosom dart
Thy shafts, and send no arrow to his heart.
I love; is it not tyranny in thee
To spare him, whilst thou giv'st such wounds to me.
Such, as my soul is sick of and I must
Die, who offend not 'cause thou art unjust.
For how is't possible I should survive
When thou diseases, and no cure will give.

Weeps.

Why should my eyes such petty griefs betray.
A heart that bleeds might weep a life away,
If it were not preserved for spite of fate,
Who thinks my sufferings of too short a date.
I must endure more misery since griefs

Will not by killing me dispense relief.
I most unhappy must retain with breath,
Griefs, which in others would be cured by death.
My grief's inflexible and will not take
The impression of those wounds which fate does make,
Though with strong torment they afflict me still,
And like hell's vengeance, torture, but not kill.

Exit floradine.

A dumb show.[22]
A temple discovered, the Duke with his lords
and attendants on the one side; on the other
Isabella and ladies. Eumenus presents her to the Duke.
A priest seems to join them. The Duke embraces her and
leads her out. Loud music and shouts within.

22. A theatrical performance in which the actors are silent, only signifying the play's action. For another example, see the "mouse-trap" scene in Shakespeare's *Hamlet* (3.2.87–258).

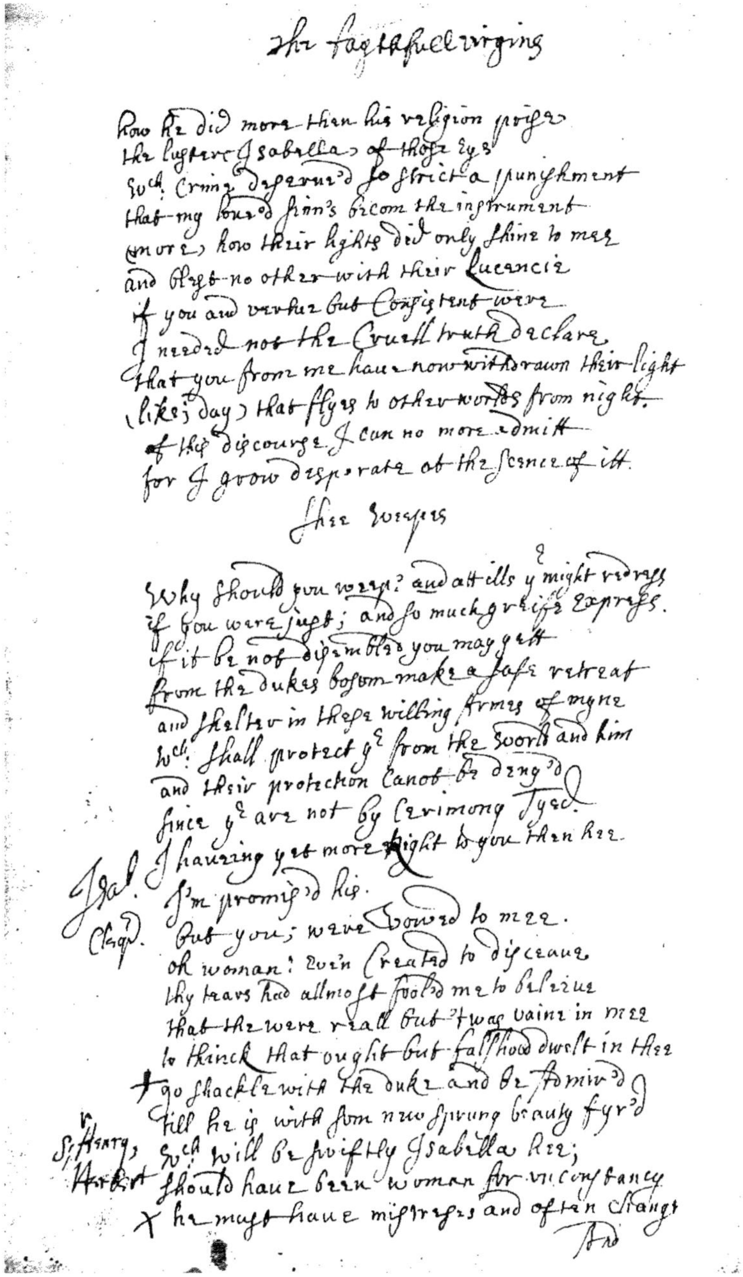

The faithfull virgins

how he did more then his religion prise
the lustre Isabella of those eys
such crime deserv'd so strict a punishment
that my lov'd shin's becom the instrument
more, how their lights did only shine to mee
and blest no other with their lucancie
if you and vertue but consistent were
I needed not the cruell truth declare
that you from me have now withdrawn their light
(like day) that flyes to other worlds from night.
of this discourse I can no more admitt
for I grow desperate at the scence of itt.

shee weepes

Why should you weep? and att ills ye might redress
if you were just; and so much greife expresse.
if it be not dissembled you may gett
from the dukes bosom make a safe retreat
and shelter in these willing armes of myne
wch shall protect ye from the world and him
and their protection canot be deny'd
since ye are not by cerimony tyed.

Isa. I having yet more right to you then hee.
I'm promis'd his.

Clag. But you; were vowed to mee.
oh woman! ev'n created to disceave
thy tears had allmost fool'd me to beleive
that the were reall but 'twas vaine in mee
to thinck that ought but falshood dwelt in thee
+ go shackle with the duke and be admir'd
till he is with som new sprung beauty fyr'd
wch will be swiftly Isabella hee;
should have been woman for inconstancy
+ he must have mistresses and often change

Sr Henry Herbert

and

Figure 6. Manuscript page of *The Faithful Virgins* with crosses and signature of Henry Herbert, Master of the Revels. Bodleian Library, Oxford. MS. Rawl. poet. 195, fol. 53v.

The Second Act

The hearse discovered. At the feet of it MERANTHA sleeping. At the head, UMIRA.

MERANTHA wakes.

MERANTHA. Why would you suffer me such rest to take,
Whilst you, my dear Umira, sigh and wake.

UMIRA. Were it not cruel in me to destroy
The sweetness which in slumber you enjoy?
Since whilst you wake both for yourself and me,
You are obliged to grieve incessantly.

MERANTHA. When both our souls shall to Elysium[23] come,
And there encounter our loved Philammon,
I cannot tell which I would wish to be
My self his once belov'd, fair nymph, or thee.

UMIRA. Should Philammon's kind spirit grateful seem
To mine, for that pure love she knows for him,
Would not Merantha's feel a jealousy?

MERANTHA. That might imply she rival were to me.
We'll smile at all that jealousy can do.
He there shall still be yours, and yet mine too.
With wreaths of lilies I will deck his head,
Whilst you with new blown roses strew his bed,
Those darling flowers which Nature holds more worth
Than all she gives the spring leave to bring forth.

UMIRA. How tedious will the swift wing'd minutes seem
'Till in the glorious shades we are with him.
What noise is that, which does our peace molest?
Can those who live in graves possess not rest?
What wanderer so weary or misled,
Would here repose him or request a bed?

Enter STATENOR, floradine, PAGE.

STATENOR. There's few would take up lodging with the dead,
'Till bold necessity compelled, but you
Who against reason sin in what you do.

23. The location of the afterlife for gods and heroes in Greek mythology, separate from the realm of Hades, the place for ordinary mortals.

UMIRA. Whom love and grief do equally subdue
May act what reason would not bend them to,
Since neither will to reason's power submit,
Each swaying mortals with more power than it.

STATENOR. Those spirits that are glorious and sublime,
With a resistless strength do govern them.
Nor love nor grief can perfect souls invade,
But by discretion both of them are swayed.

UMIRA. Of that, Sir, we will not discourse of here,
Since love and it incompatible are.

STATENOR. You seem most just in what you now declare.
If reason or discretion governed you,
You'd leave this place and quit your passion too.
Not vainly over dead Philammon grieve,
As though your tears again could make him live,
Who sits with clouds and smiles at you below,
And had he blood would blush at what you do.
He was a noble youth, but did not seem
From you to merit what you pay to him.

MERANTHA throws up her veil.

MERANTHA. Philammon did so much deserve that she
'Till death division makes will sigh with me
His loss. We mutually have vowed to mourn,
'Till age or sorrow calls us to an urn.
Whence though our bodies never might remove,
Our souls shall swiftly fly to him we love.

STATENOR gazes at her. She veils again.

floradine. (Aside) Though to my brother's dust I ought to pay
My sighs and tears with passion great as they,
A grief more forcibly does me surprise
To see Statenor wounded by those eyes.
Love over Nature does the mastery get,
And sways my bosom with more strength than it.

STATENOR. Why should you hide more than the world can boast
Beneath that cloud?

floradine. (Aside) Oh, he is ever lost—

STATENOR. Draw that black curtain and thy light display,
And let thy beams outshine the soul of day.

MERANTHA. The light I have must show itself to none,
But sit here in the shade of Philammon.

STATENOR. Heaven will not permit it. A sun so bright
Should with a prosp'rous influence bless the sight
Of us poor mortals, who in shade must die,
If thus you veil its luster from the eye
Of all that live. But you'll grow less severe,
And with your rays the souls of mankind clear,
Not in eclipse involve your beauties here.

floradine. (Aside) Oh heaven, that tongue may charm a vestal's ear.

MERANTHA. Be not, Sir, of opinion to believe
That in this world I can do ought but grieve.

STATENOR. You cannot to the world so cruel prove
And to your self. You must not grieve but love.

MERANTHA. Here constantly I will both love and grieve.

STATENOR. You must love me, fair virgin, that dost live.

MERANTHA. Leave me. I do conjure you. What you've said
Is injurious to me and to the dead,
Whose merit you make slight since you suspect,
That I staying in the world would ere reject
His relic, I bemoan, all it does own
Cannot make up another Philammon.

STATENOR. 'Tis evident you never loved but one,
And only knew the worth of him alone.
If you would frame your soul to love again,
You might find one as worthy of your flame,
As ever Philammon did seem to be,
Whose love you do deplore so faithfully.

MERANTHA.[24] To your discourse I must no more give ear.
You're speaking what is guilt in me to hear.

STATENOR. Since all that I can urge wants force to move
You, Madam, to incline again to love,

24. The manuscript assigns this speech to "Umira," but as this makes little sense, the speech prefix has been changed to "Merantha," since it is she whom Statenor is courting. Umira is his sister.

I will offend you with entreats no more
To grant what I must but in vain implore.
Yet one request I'll humbly make to you.

MERANTHA. Before I grant, tell me for what you sue.

STATENOR. 'Tis that you still would hide that taking light,
Which must not shine to me, from human sight.
What you have shown I so admire and love,
That I of rivalry shall too jealous prove,
And jealousy to lovers is more pain,
Than to support a mistress's disdain.
Did every mortal know what heaven were,
Mankind would study naught but to get there,
But being ignorant of what it is,
We place our happiness in meaner bliss.
If Statenor had not your beauty seen,
Another might, as you have, vanquished him.
But you appear so strong a conqueror,
That he can ne'er submit to other power.
Make no reply, too sensibly I feel.
Your eyes but wound me but your words do kill.
For all that you do utter I declare
But animates your lover to despair,
And what is he that can despair and live.
Men can no longer than they hope survive.
Sister, with bright Merantha, you may stay
Whilst I will hence, and sigh a life away,
Cause she will still a lover dead prefer,
For whom she grieves, but I must die for her.

floradine. Oh heaven, how passionate he seems to be.
My sorrows, death can only remedy.

Enter a GENTLEMAN.

GENTLEMAN. The Duke, my lord, hath sent in haste for you.

STATENOR. I have not paid what should from me be due
To him. Sir, I will instantly attend
His Highness. Will you but once more descend
To let me see your face. But do not. You,
By granting that would but my wound renew.
I hither came to persuade you away.
Now here I would my self forever stay.

Exit STATENOR, floradine, GENTLEMAN.

MERANTHA. Let sleeping embraces clasp you, noblest maid.
From soft repose you have too long been stayed.

UMIRA. No, my Merantha. I must sigh and wake,
To think of that unhappy conquest which you make
Over my brother's heart, which ne'er 'till now
To beauty did submit, I dare avow.
Would it from other eyes had taken flame,
Since that it took from you might burn in vain.

MERANTHA. Is't possible that tears should flames emit,
Or water fire produce 'twas never yet
In nature. Can my showery eyes have power
Think you to inspire a flame in Statenor?

UMIRA. The sun through clouds and showers does glorious show,
As through your blacks and tears your beauties do.
Beauty and sorrow both in you do move
Hearts to incline to pity and to love.
As bosoms do soften with your tears,
Your charming eyes, the soul of man endears.
To dote upon your grief did ne'er appear
So sweet in any shape as it does here
In my Merantha.

MERANTHA. I with tears implore
Umira on this theme to speak no more.

UMIRA. In silence I my brother's fate deplore.

MERANTHA. Repose you in the downy arms of sleep.
'Tis more than time that I should watch and weep.

The hearse shut in.

Enter CLEOPHON as in a grove looking about. On the side of it, a cave discovered.

CLEOPHON. Sure in this dismal place those hags do live—
Which only can a satisfaction give
Me of my fate. Who does inhabit here? (He knocks.)

Enter two witches.

I find I'm right by those which now appear.

First witch. Speak thy desires, most noble Cleophon.
Thou canst not ask, the thing shall not be done
That lies within the compass of our art,
And therefore freely what you wish, impart.

Cleophon. You promise fairly and I will be brief.
Is it in you to give a soul relief,
That is afflicted with despair and love.
Let this to me your kindnesses improve,
And if within the limits of your art,
Slay the anguish of a wounded heart.

First witch. Sir, you in love have had such ill success,
That 'tis not in our power now to redress
The ills you suffer because much too late,
You've made your wishes known, nor is't in Fate
For to revenge a sentence she hath passed.

Cleophon. Your words give me a pain too great to last.
For death, no doubt, will instantly ensue,
And cure the wounds which I receive from you.

First witch. Stay. We as far as magic will proceed.

They charm.

Second witch. By the waving of this reed,
You knowing ministers from earth arise,
But in such forms as may allure our eyes.

Two Spirits ascend in white, like nymphs.

Spirit. Speak why we here are summoned by you
From our secure abodes. What must we do?

witch. Tell me, shall noble Cleophon possess
Her he most loves?

Spirit. Never. That happiness
He knows another's destined to enjoy.

Cleophon. He that feels all death's plagues but once can die.

Spirit. We have answered thy demands and cannot stay
One minute longer.

witch. Hence away; away.

witch stamps and SPIRITS descend.

witch. I will conjure the spirits of the air
Straight to descend. They much more knowing are.

Exit witch.

Thunder as in the air; as that eases, soft music and a song. Song ended and spirits in the shape of men and women descend and dance. Which being done, all vanish.[25]

FIRST witch. Will they not speak?

SECOND witch. No. But I'll summon those
Which can the deepest mysteries disclose.

Exit witch.

Music again as in the air. Three aerial SPIRITS descend, and re-enter witch.

FIRST SPIRIT. Why are we so charmed for to appear below?

SECOND SPIRIT. And what are thy commands?

THIRD SPIRIT. Speak. Let us know.

witch. The fate of Cleophon unfold to me.

FIRST SPIRIT. Cleophon shall be prince of Tuscany.

CLEOPHON. Ha!

witch. Silence, Sir. Tell me before you go
Shall he enjoy her he most loves?

SECOND SPIRIT. Oh no—

THIRD SPIRIT. An hour shall come in which he shall despise
The Beauty which he now so much does prize.

The SPIRITS ascend in the scene.

CLEOPHON. Why would you suffer them to vanish hence,
Leaving me in the torture of suspense.
Cannot you force them to appear again,
And tell me how I shall be duke, or when.
And what can e're induce me to condemn
Her that in spite of falsehood I esteem?

25. Much as the stage direction in Shakespeare's *The Tempest* (4.1.138).

WITCH. No. The next moon we will our charms renew,
And then what you request unfold to you.

CLEOPHON. Here. (Gives gold.) To your kindness I'm a debtor still.

WITCH. It shall our practice be to serve your will.

CLEOPHON. You must some thanks, my friends, from me receive.
'Till I can nobler recompenses give.

Exit severally.[26]

Enter FLORADINE *solus.*[27]

FLORADINE. By him I love I am obliged to sue
Against myself and my dead brother too
To her, who does so constantly deplore
His loss, I must for Statenor implore.

Studies awhile.[28]

To fair Merantha who so just appears,
She makes his ashes famous by her tears.
She loved, and noblest lovers do frequent,
As some bless'd shrine Philammon's monument.
But I from him my soul could much more prize,
Than all the wealth that in the bosom lies
Of the rich ocean, to my ruin must
Persuade her to reject Philammon's dust,
To love my Statenor and cease to grieve,
But I cannot do that and think to live.

Studies again.

And yet I will. Merantha cannot be
From faith perverted to inconstancy.
Her matchless soul temptation will despise.
I am secure where so much virtue is.
Her rivalship I shall not need to fear.
For she I know will none alive prefer.

Exit.

26. Separately.

27. Latin for "alone."

28. Pauses to think.

The Third Act

Two GENTLEMEN discovered preparing seats for the DUKE and DUCHESS.

FIRST GENTLEMAN. What is't the masquers do present tonight?

SECOND GENTLEMAN. Somewhat in virtue's praise not worth our sight.

FIRST GENTLEMAN. Virtue's disgraced; we should not use her name.
That would be *à la mode*[29] and price our fame.
A piteous, wretched, out of fashion thing,
Scorned now as much by beggar as by . . .

Enter a GENTLEMAN in haste.

THIRD GENTLEMAN. The masquers are already to appear.
Dispatch. The DUKE is upon entering here.

Flourish.

EUMENUS, STATENOR, TRASILIUS, CLEON bearing[30] the DUKE. DUCHESS, ATTENDANTS, COURTIERS.
DUKE and DUCHESS take their places.

The Masque

Enter at one door: ENVY. At another: DETRACTION.[31] They meet and embrace.

ENVY. Detraction!

DETRACTION. Dearest Envy, let us kiss.
Ha! We are interrupted. Who is this?

Enter AMBITION strutting in great state.[32] After him LECHERY attended by two PAGES.

29. French for "in fashion" or "up to date."

30. Carrying him, probably on a chair.

31. Disparagement or belittling; the opposite of attraction; a lessening of reputation through criticism.

32. With much self-importance.

ENVY. Ambition's self. Let us awhile stand by.

DETRACTION. What's he that follows?

ENVY. Oh, t'is Lechery.

They retire to a corner of the stage.

AMBITION. Dear Lechery, what remains for us to do
On earth, we can but all the world subdue,
And that I think is near perfection done.

LECHERY. No millions triumph, that have us o'ercome.
Sirha, go fetch me straight a handsome whore.
One will not satisfy. I must have more.
Yet bring but Pride. I will each hour have fresh.
Sure there's no heaven like this sin of flesh.
To lie clasped in a mistress's soft arms,
Whose every touch our souls in pleasures charms,
Whose looks are sweetness and whose eyes are fire,
Which brightly kindle and supply desire.

Studies.

AMBITION. Sirha, bid Flattery attend me here.
Of her designs I must with her confer.

Exit PAGE.

LECHERY. Why should not she I so much wish appear.

Enter CHASTITY in white with her hair disheveled, with a wreath of lilies upon her head.

ENVY. What is that gay white shining thing that enters there?
Her that his soul covets so much to see?

DETRACTION. All curses on her. No, it's Chastity,
A slighted nymph; one men hate perfectly,
And women too, in this age that are wise,
They're foul or fools, that such a trifle prize.

LECHERY spies CHASTITY.

LECHERY. Ha! What malicious fury sent thee here?
Hence from my sight and never more appear

To offend my eyes, which had much rather see
Death in all horrors, than one glimpse of thee.

CHASTITY. Oh where shall I inhabit? Cruelly
The world denies a being now to me.

Enter an ANGEL, who spreads his wings over her, and takes her and seats her at the DUCHESS's feet.

ANGEL. Whilst virgin here thou ever shalt abide,
And favor find from this illustrious bride,
Whose virtue always will propitious be
To that unsullied glory shrined in thee.

Enter PAGE with PRIDE.

LECHERY. The idol of my soul approaches now.
Tell me, rare miracle of excellence, how
I should adore thee. Heavens, how fair she is—

ENVY. Detraction, what strange painted puppet's this?

DETRACTION. 'Tis Pride, a wench, mistress to Lechery.

LECHERY. Come, my Beloved. On beds of roses we
Will dial the hours away, and joyously prove
All blisses fancied in the joys of Love—

Enter PAGE with FLATTERY.

AMBITION. Welcome, dear Flattery, I in thee profess
All that frail man on earth calls happiness.

FLATTERY. I'm in your favor blessed.

AMBITION. Thy brows I'll deck
With gems more rich than e're adorned the neck
Of the admired and famous Cyprian queen[33]—
One careless smile of thine shall ev'n redeem
Monarchs from bondage, that will subdue.

FLATTERY. The gods may fear to be o'ercome by you.

LECHERY. Let us to our desired enjoyments haste,
Not uselessly the precious minutes waste.

33. A reference to Aphrodite (Venus), goddess of love; one of her cult centers was Cyprus.

PRIDE. Best servant, you shall ever find that I
With your desires will readily comply.
But I with Flattery, by whose influence
I live, must needs confer, e're I go hence,
About some things that touch my bosom near.

Goes to FLATTERY and embraces her.

FLATTERY. How much you honor your idolater,
Bright Lady. Whilst your arms enfold me thus,
Me thinks the gods themselves grow envious
At my felicity.

PRIDE. The gods by me,
Must ne'er be worshipped, Flattery, like thee.
But I too long neglect to pay what's due
To my Great Father.

Kneels to AMBITION, who takes her up.

PRIDE. Kings must stoop to you.
Permit me then, Sir, on my knees to show
What homage both the world and I do owe
Your greatness—

Offers to kneel again.

AMBITION. Rise. You must not kneel to me.
Pride should at least Ambition's equal be.

Enter AVARICE, with DRUNKENNESS reeling in after him.

AVARICE. Thou in superfluous drafts consums't my store.
Thy brother, Lechery, on a costly whore
Misspends the treasure which with so much pain
I from my youth have labored to attain.
Both the widow and the fatherless,
For your ungracious sakes do still oppress
Despite their tears, when they for mercy sue,
To pile up wealth, which wasted is by you.

DRUNKENNESS sings.

AVARICE. The plague of ill-got riches lights on me,
In both of you, you sons of infamy.

DRUNKENNESS. What is't the power of sack wants force to do,
Fools it makes wise, and cowards valiant too.

LECHERY. To lie, Sir, in a mistress's embrace,
Whose language is as charming as her face,
Upon whose cheeks roses so fresh appear,
That you would swear eternal spring dwelt there.
Whose voice and lute used by her hand is such
As ravishes our souls at every touch—
Are pleasures, Sir, that you did never know,
Or you would better far of them allow.

DRUNKENNESS. Some music, boy, and call my comrades in.
We'll sing and dance, and loose our cares in wine.

BOY brings in five more as drunken, who join and dance the swift measure.

LECHERY. This music has allured my senses too—
Why should not I all that delights pursue?
Throw by, Sir, your severity awhile,
And mark with how much sweetness we beguile
Old time of minutes, which too swiftly pass
From us, whilst her with holding of our glass
Grows weary—He that would gain dominion (to AVARICE)
Must with a free and cheerful soul march on
Toward victory; such as dully move,
Are never blessed in empire nor in love.
To grace our measure you must not deny.
I will take Pride. You shall have Flattery.
What can a gay and aerie soul transcend,
Come. They shall make us out which us attend.

AMBITION. Such wanton sports suit not with thoughts like mine.
The fall of kings, by which I hope to climb
Aloft to empire, can deliver me.

FLATTERY. Compliance is the life of policy.
Princes, Sir, oft their vassals' wills obey.
A feigned humility's the statesman's key,
Wherewith he does unlock the people's breast,
And he most prospers that dissembles best.

Besides, to Lechery some respect is due,
He ruling now more parts o'th world than you.

DETRACTION. To Flattery's counsel he an ear doth bend
To all she wishes he does condescend.

ENVY. Flattery does great Ambition animate
To high achievements and designs of state.
With Envy he from her receives,
Who most securely in his bosom lives.

DETRACTION. List! For their active measure they prepare.
Behold with what equality the pair.
Ambition, he has chosen Flattery,
And Pride is taken out by Lechery.
And Treason couples with his brother Sloth.
Oh, for the Devil to take Avarice forth.

They join and dance the second measure.

Enter VIRTUE and ATTENDANTS.

ENVY. Inform me, what is she approaches now?

DETRACTION. Virtue! Humility and Patience too.
Attend her, by their habits you may see
How little in this age they valued be.

AMBITION looks sternly at VIRTUE.

AMBITION. What make you here? Hence from my presence fly.

PRIDE. She is a foe to me—

LECHERY. My enemy.

FLATTERY. Fair unblemished light—

VIRTUE. Away. Thou art unpleasing to my sight.
The seraphs aloud my praises sing,
And when I'm named, each cherub claps his wing.
This by instinct I know, but know that I
Condemn the hyperboles of Flattery.

AMBITION. I can no longer with her stay. Dispense—

She[34] goes and seats herself by CHASTITY at the DUCHESS's feet.

34. Virtue.

VIRTUE. Here I will shelter from your violence.
Here Virtue shall a safe protection find,
Where Honor sways each soul, Glory the mind.
These will to me their favors still incline.
Both high and bright examples, and do seem
My greatest lights for none do blaze like them.

AMBITION and the rest gaze at VIRTUE.

AMBITION. Ambition would reject all he held here
Of late, and would decline it to live there.

LECHERY. Who would not lust and wantonness despise
To be advanced where spotless Virtue is.

PRIDE. Would her vanities condemn and hate,
Could she but hope t' attain so blest a fate.

FLATTERY. And on that score, what would not Flattery do.

DUKE. If all turn virtuous, I'll grow sober too,
Presuming I may be as blest as you.

VIRTUE. Refined from vice, exalted you shalt be
To honors here and glory share with me.

They all bow to VIRTUE.

AVARICE. Avarice does now to you himself submit.

ENVY. Avarice! I am much more surprised at it
Than at the change I was of these before.
And his conversion does rejoice me more.
My very priests by Avarice were misled.
Here's miracle beyond what ere was read.
This nymph's worthy of your kindness too.

OMNES. That untouched virgin we adore in you.

VIRTUE. There's something due from me to this white day,
Which I and my associates will pay.

Enter JUSTICE, PRUDENCE, SOBRIETY.

VIRTUE. See Justice, Prudence, and Sobriety,
Chastity, Patience, and Humility.

JUSTICE. The vices which so ruled I've vanquished now.
Let this triumphant wreath impale thy brow.

JUSTICE crowns VIRTUE with a wreath.

The ANGEL takes CHASTITY, who with VIRTUE and her ASSOCIATES dance the third measure.[35]

ENVY. Amongst so many virtues that are here,
I wonder Charity does not appear.

DETRACTION. A deadly ague has taken hold of her,
And she is now so weak she cannot stir.
But let us hence.

ENVY. 'Tis wisely urged by you.
For if we stay, we shall turn virtuous too.

VIRTUE addresses her[36] to the DUKE and DUCHESS.

VIRTUE. My conquest, Princes, I ascribe to you.
And humbly at your feet, my laurel throw.
Virtue with so much luster does appear
To shine in you, that Vice admiring her there,
To make these converts, my attempts have been
Fruitless—and all endeavors lost on them,
But that they extasied with wonder see
How amiable I am in majesty,
Where they adore me, and will practice how
To stay'n your favors, and grow Virtue's now.

Exeunt omnes.

Finis masque.

35. A slow and stately dance.

36. That is, herself.

The Fourth Act

Enter STATENOR and floradine.

floradine. As ice touched by a warm hand melts, so she
Did softer seem.

STATENOR. Ha! Then she pitied me.

floradine. Yes Sir.

STATENOR. Oh, that her charity might prove.
Such saints oft pity those they cannot love.
The gods did make her fair above her kind.
And beauty equaled with as bright a mind,
Whose outward form they did not only grace,
But made her soul as alluring as her face.
'Tis that, my floradine, endears my heart
Beyond all charms that beauty can impart.

floradine. Though she to cure the wounds she makes declines,
Yet know such justice in her bosom shines,
That she declares so much to you is due,
That next the dead, she will love none but you.

STATENOR. I'm in this cruel kindness more unblessed,
Than if she had my flames with scorn suppressed.

Studies.

floradine. (Aside) By what he now declares too well I see,
That he, alas, is ever lost to me.

floradine weeps and sighs.

STATENOR. Ha! Thus heaven's tears hang on the new blown flowers,
And so sun does mingle beams with showers.
Must my ill fate in love create in thee
A sorrow to augment the misery
I feel in it? Oh spare these precious drops sweet boy.
They have not power to soften destiny.
Come, dry thy eyes, what should this passion move
In thee whose youth is unconcerned in Love.
But if so early that hath touched thy breast
What is she that can thy soft charms resist?

floradine. No woman, Sir, can e're my breast subdue.
These only flow to express my love to you.

Statenor. I have observed thy kindness still to me,
Above what I can e're requite in thee.

foradine. Oh no. All that poor floradine can do
Will scarce amount to gratitude to you
For favors past. Besides, even in excess
You shower new bounties, and my debt excrease
To your high worth, which I could wish were less.

Statenor. How floradine?

floradine. Be not surprised[37] for I
Upon your unmatched goodness so rely,
That I grow free and to presume to say
What ere an open soul, Sir, would display.
(Aside) How near am I my passion to betray.

Statenor. Why shouldst thou be so great an enemy
To wish my honor or my worth from me,
The only treasures that enrich a mind.
In this thou seemst malicious and unkind.
Have I not loved thee more than princes' health?
And looked upon thee as my chiefest wealth,
Embosomed thee here in this luckless breast,
Where next the fair Merantha thou art placed?

floradine. By what you now relate I find I'm more
Obliged than I conceived myself before
To noble Statenor, whose merit favors were
Above my merit still, I must declare.
But I perceive they now so far extend,
That nothing can my sense of them transcend.
Did it not, prudence and great thrift appear
In me, to wish that you less worthy were?
For had not, Sir, your worth so matchless been,
I should not so unblessed and wretched seem
As now I must, who ne'er can pay to you,
My favors presage, the least of what I owe.
Above all griefs that e're oppress me yet,
I grieve to think that I must die in debt.

37. The manuscript here reads "Be not surprised" twice in the line. As this seems in error, the first "Be not surprised" has been omitted.

STATENOR. Thy taking rhetoric cannot choose but move
The bright Merantha to incline to love,
For questionless my floradine can woo
Her as Philammon could never do.
Thou shalt to her again, but I advise
Thee not to dare to gaze upon her eyes.
Thou wilt be lost if thou those glories view,
Nor list to ought she says—

floradine. What must I do,
My lord, with one that I must not see or hear,
Whisper my love in sighs in her chaste ear?
And in thy winningest language I couth relate
My sufferings 'till she grows compassionate,
And beg of her for to make no reply
Except she will with my dying comply?
Her language is as charming as her face,
And there's such harmony in all she says
As if both heaven and nature meant that she,
Should every way o're hearts victorious be.

Studies.

STATENOR. Ha! It is dangerous to send thee there.
Thy graces may a captive make of her.

floradine. Oh, do not harbor such a jealousy.
There's nothing, Sir, that can attract in me.

STATENOR. You do not see so much as I discry,
But I'll on thy unblemished faith rely.
Go, hasten to her, and from me express
All that seems likely to procure redress.
Tell her those flames her eyes emitted here,
Grow more impetuous than at first they were.
And farther add, the fires which I derive
From them, in justice she should keep alive.

Exit STATENOR. *Manet*[38] floradine.

floradine. This cruel imposition wounds me more,
Than all the shafts of love could here before.
Oh, how perverse and rigid is the fate

38. Latin for "remains" or "stays."

Which rules me. Must I be an advocate
Against myself. For him I love and sue
In's[39] cause to her that is my rival too.
Both love and fate my ruin sure conspire,
And I must envy her I do admire,
The kind and just Merantha to whose eyes,
My Statenor will only sacrifice.
But why at her should I malicious be,
That is a miracle of constancy,
Or let my passion rage to jealousy.
Love's frenzy and the fortune of each soul,
It does invade. I must betimes control
The power it usurpeth in my breast,
Whilst it by reason's force me be suppressed.
Yet all that are by love inspired, like me
Must know and feel the pain of jealousy.

Studies.

Should I to Statenor disclose my flame,
I might more wretched be than now I am.
My idle dotage he must sure condemn,
And much despise. Besides 'tis given to men
To hate and slight those which most dote on them.
No. I am safe and free in this disguise,
And him I love is still within my eyes,
And those commands which he does on me lay,
'Tis fit I should implicitly obey.
That way my flame will with most luster shine,
And I shall merit, though I have not him.

Exit floradine.

Enter TRASILIUS and the DUCHESS.

TRASILIUS. Umira, like a glorious stream of light,
Dazzled his ravished senses at first sight.
Her beauty, Madame, full as much has done
As yours can act, who are indeed our sun.
The heart your brighter eyes did once subdue,
And was a conquest only fit for you,

39. Probably a contraction for "in his."

Is by another victoress ore'come.
Madame, this truth throughout the country known.

DUCHESS. Since Tuscany so lately did incline,
To worship none like to these eyes of mine,
Which do retain their vaunted luster still,
I cannot think this is a truth, nor will—

TRASILIUS. Madame, with sighs I wish that he may seem
To merit what your virtue thinks of him.

Enter the DUKE, who takes no notice of his DUCHESS but walks off again.

DUKE. Ha! This is strange, and I begin to fear
That 'tis no less than truth which I do hear.

Exit DUCHESS.

TRASILIUS. She's gone and with her my felicity.
How cruel and averse is destiny,
With a strange rigor that does me pursue,
And love like destiny afflicts me too,
Who never could against a breast design,
A mischief like to that he aims at mine,
Compelling me to dote on her, whom I
Must ne'er presume to hope I shall enjoy.
What can the anguish of a heart remove
Where even despair more empire has than love.

Enter FRANCISCUS.

FRANCISCUS. What griefs can your noble mind oppress,
And indispose you thus even to excess?

TRASILIUS. Let me in whisper breathe my griefs to thee.

Whisper.

FRANCISCUS. You know not how compassionate she'll be
Because you have not courage, Sir, to try.

TRASILIUS. I could, Franciscus, with more courage die
What deaths from her just scorn I might receive.
Ere dare to show it I will cease to live.

FRANCISCUS. Vouchsafe[40] me hearing—

TRASILIUS. Urge it not for I,
To my last bed will swift in silence fly.
Insensible we lie in Death's cold arms,
All Love's tyranny and Beauty's charms,
Whose flames that to excess torment us here,
Lose all their vigor, and grow frozen there,
In his eternal winter, where we rest
Secure from all rude griefs that can molest.
Prithee, what news?

FRANCISCUS. The Duke is newly gone
Into death's shade to worship a bright sun,
The fair Umira, who in clouds and tears,
The enamored soul of Tuscany endears,
And he with love, and passion courts her too.

TRASILIUS[41] studies.

TRASILIUS. Why should not I as well as he pursue
My love. There's not twixt [us] such inequality,
But I may warrant mine as well as he.
And since his frailty teaches us to sin,
Who dare reproach us, whilst we act like him.
But oh, the Duchess's virtue is so great
That I from her, might fear a sad defeat.

FRANCISCUS. Her virtue faulty was to Cleophon.

TRASILIUS. Within I will consult what's to be done.
Those wounds her beauty makes in justice she
Should cure, if not what will become of me.

Exit.

The hearse discovered. UMIRA, MERANTHA, floradine.

MERANTHA. Did not thy sex convince me, I'd believe
My Erasila were come here to grieve
Her brother's loss, which I might still deplore.

40. "Grant" or "permit" me.

41. The manuscript here reads "Statenor," but as this character is not on stage, it is Trasilius who should have this stage direction.

FLORADINE. (Aside) I must admit of this discourse no more.
Lest I myself too visibly betray.
Will you vouchsafe to hear what I should say?

MERANTHA. Yes. So you'll promise not to treat of love.

FLORADINE. I dare not, Madame. I'm obliged to move
Such business only to your gentle ear.

MERANTHA. All thoughts of love in me lie buried here.

FLORADINE. Though love too powerfully can enslave
Our souls, whilst we on earth a being have,
His power grows useless when we hence remove.
The dead, who die to all things, die to love,
And he's insensible whom you bemoan
Of all the glory you have to him done.
Therefore, prepare you to receive a flame,
From one that lives, Madame, and can love again,
The noble Statenor, who did despise
All love could act, until he saw your eyes.
But now, vanquished by them, resists no more
The charms of beauty, nor love's greater power.
Though with resistless force he did subdue
All love could act, and powerful beauty too,
'Till he was conquered, and o'rcome by you.

MERANTHA. Ah, hadst thou known his worth whose loss I mourn,
Thou would not court me to forsake his urn
To love another, which I ne'er can do.
And you for Statenor but vainly sue.

FLORADINE. Fame does report that he for whom I sigh
Consistent was with all things great and high,
Whilst Heaven permitted him to sojourn here.
But now his nobler port inhabits there,
And o're his worst remains 'tis that ye grieve,
Wasting on them what's due to those that live,
Your youth and beauty, which do blessings seem
To living, Madame, but not to dead men.
Consider how that fabric ruined is,
Which when 'twas perfect you did justly grieve.

MERANTHA. Though but his ruined fabric here remains,
I'll in his ashes keep alive that flame,

Wherewith at first Love did my heart inspire,
Where it shall blaze, sweet youth, 'till I expire.

floradine. What fire can blaze, Madame, that does not receive
Some heat to feed it, or how can it live?

MERANTHA. Where Love once truly burns so clear, I doubt
It ne'er will be extinguished or put out.
But in some breasts he makes so short a stay,
That he like lightning visits and away.
But he such empire hath achieved in mine,
That whilst I am, he there will flame and shine.
Though the effect that caused him first is gone,
He'll live while I can think of Philammon.

floradine.[42] But, Madame, what might brave Statenor do,
A wretched martyr fall to Love and you.
Enough from you and more than's due you've paid
Unto the memory of a lover dead.
Let him that lives and loves you pity find.
Will you to none but to the dead be kind?
As fame extols your matchless constancy,
It will accuse you of severity.
If you to Statenor thus cruel seem,
What woman ist but you would love him?

floradine sighs.

MERANTHA. I pity him.

floradine. Philosophy does prove
Compassion the original of Love.
The man you pity sure you cannot hate.
But you must love what you compassionate.

MERANTHA. No, those we pity we can oft despise,
And even compassionate our enemies.

Enter the DUKE with PAGES and ATTENDANTS. He addresses himself to UMIRA. floradine aside seems to confer with MERANTHA. The ATTENDANTS wait at distance.

42. Here the manuscript indicates "Merantha," but clearly the lines belong to floradine, as it makes no sense for Merantha to address floradine, whom she thinks is a male page, as "Madame."

DUKE. Will you still cruelly eclipse your light,
And not dispense one ray to bless my sight?
But that which you would hide you cannot shroud.
The glorious sun through a concealing cloud,
Discovers luster, and his beams does show,
As through that veil your wondrous beauties do.
Though the Egyptians, Madame, as we read,
Place tapers in the caverns of the dead,
No story says that beauty e're did flame
In vaults or urns until you hither came.

UMIRA. 'Tis love, not beauty, Sir, that does shine here.

DUKE. Both, Madame, both. But this is not their sphere.
But to be brief, will you to court remove,
Where you more properly may shine and love.

UMIRA. No, never, Sir. Here I will stay 'til Death
Compels me to resign to him my breath.

DUKE. This is a strange resolve. Why should you stay?
He sighs your beauty and your youth away.
Here at the tomb of Philammon who to
The sweet Merantha did pretend, not you.
Their nuptial was decreed, and the fair bride
Prepared to be by sacred ceremony tied
In holy wedlock. Death the bridegroom took,
And left the maid abandoned and forsook,
In him whose loss she ought much to bemoan
As having cause. But, Madame, you have none.

UMIRA. Sir, I shall reason show for what I do,
When I declared I loved Philammon too.
And I do freely now that passion own,
Which had he lived the air should ne'er have known.
And in my grief my love shall still be shown.

DUKE. What Love's resistless power has wrought in you,
In me he acts, and I must love you too.
That power designs it whom no force controls,
That does enslave our hearts and rule our souls.

UMIRA. Virtue forbid that you should sacrifice
Your love to other than the Duchess's eyes.

DUKE. Hers I confess prevailed, 'till yours I see,
Over my heart, but yours now vanquish me

With greater force than hers could ever do.
My breast they captive and my soul subdue.

UMIRA. I must of this discourse no more admit.
Be pleased to cease it, and love where 'tis fit
You should. Your beauteous Duchess, Sir, I mean.

DUKE. All you can urge can ne'er my heart reclaim
From that wild passion which your eyes create,
Which you must lessen and extenuate
By your dispensing what I most desire,
For as you have kindled, you must feed my fire.

UMIRA. I all respect and duty shall throw by,
If, Sir, you do proceed thus viciously.

DUKE. You cannot frown me from my love. 'Twill flame
Higher like sparks by wind storms will. Distain
Not to be troublesome. I'll leave you now
For to consider what you ought to do.
My bosom, Madame, has tak'n fire from you.
Where 'tis your part to feed and quench it too.

UMIRA. 'Tis lust, not I, that your ill fire hath made.
In saying you did, I the truth displayed.

DUKE. I must pursue my passions to the height.
You have my soul. The Duchess but my faith.

Exit DUKE, ATTENDANTS. UMIRA goes weeping, toward MERANTHA.

UMIRA. Oh! my Merantha.

MERANTHA. Ha! Why are these tears?

UMIRA. They spring from sorrow, and my softer fears.
The wanton Duke so vicious does appear
That what I have to say will wound thy ear.

MERANTHA. But Statenor does so much worthy seem
That I resent his griefs and pity him.

UMIRA. Let us retire, and I'll to you relate
How love against me does conspire with fate.

The scene is closed.[43]

43. The phrasing of the stage direction here seems unusually specific, perhaps to draw attention to the use of shutters such that the opening of the next act might dramatically emphasize the situation of the Duchess. See Introduction, p. 19.

The Fifth Act

Chairs set out upon the stage by PAGES.

Enter EUMENUS, CLEON, and the DUCHESS.

EUMENUS. Freely to me your discontents declare.
I must partaker be of what they are.

CLEON. Where griefs by force kept prisoner in a breast,
It peace destroys, and robs the soul of rest.
But once enlarged, it can no more oppress
A bosom nor afflict it to excess.

DUCHESS. Then briefly, I'll to both of you reveal
That which I have not power to conceal
One minute longer. Let my tears win sway.

EUMENUS. This takes my wonder. Heavens; what sooth you say.

She wipes her eyes.

DUCHESS. Is't possible, my lords, you should not see
How I neglected am by Tuscany.
If you discern not how I slighted am,
It is my wonder you're not told by Fame
Who speaks it loudly. It not whispered is.
He loves Umira, and does me despise.
This is a grief which I cannot support.

EUMENUS. He often does where she abides resort.
But she is virtuous, and you need not fear.
For his ill love must prove successless there.
She ever owned a white unsullied fame.
But I the Duke must for his folly blame.

DUCHESS. All you can urge can ne'er his heart reclaim.

CLEON. Madame, he may be told that he does err.
I'll take the privilege of a counselor.
Besides, it is my duty to advise
His youth, ere he to fame and honor dies,
Which he will swiftly, if he thus pursue
What lust, the shame of Nature, leads him to.

DUCHESS. I wish he may to your advice submit.
He cannot err whilst he is swayed by it,
But he to frenzy does Umira love,
And all you say must ineffectual prove.

EUMENUS. If for a time you can disguise your grief,
Be confident it shall have swift relief.

DUCHESS. Teach me how I should such a grief disguise,
That is disclosed both by my heart and eyes,
Being equally betrayed by fears and sighs.

CLEON. Madame, awhile you must your tears restrain,
Though it is grief's diversion to complain.

DUCHESS. What you would have me shroud I cannot hide.

EUMENUS. You do not know because you have not tried.
You swiftly must yourself experiment.
The wise dissemble ills which they resent,
Such ills as are unfit to be revealed.
In my opinion, yours should be concealed,
Whilst we endeavor with all care and art
For to reclaim th'affections of his heart.

DUCHESS. I to the utmost of my strength will try
How far I can, with that you wish comply.
To all that you advise me I should bow,
Who of your counsel cannot disallow.
'Tis that must save me, and I will obey.

EUMENUS. You now express what I would have you say.
Let those bold griefs that do your peace molest
Be unto Cleon or to me expressed.
Let them to none but to our bosoms fly,
Who will design to give them remedy.

DUCHESS. What you enjoin, infallibly I'll do,
And will my sorrows only sigh to you.
(Aside) My vengeance my fair rival shall pursue,
And if Trasilius promise keep with me.

EUMENUS. Now we'll commit you to your privacy.

Exit severally.

Enter TRASILIUS, pensive.

TRASILIUS. Ha! Let me think what love would make me do,
Destroy a woman and a beauty too.
'Tis a strange act, a crime I should abhor,
But 'tis the will of her, whom I adore,
And I must her commands dispute no more.

Studies.

What devil is't that rages in my blood,
And totally does ruin all that's good
And great within my bosom. I will die
Ere blot my soul with such an infamy,
But I lose all my hopes if I deny.
Besides the moving Duchess did infer
That by rude force the Duke would ruin her.
That sin would light on him; but this on me.
And I in acting it must wretched be.

Studies again.

Where lust supremacy gets in a soul,
Virtue and virtue's force it does control.
It makes me ills which I despise pursue,
And leads me to a crime I hate to do.

Exit.

Enter the DUKE with three or four disguised.

ONE. At the back stairs shall we your coming wait.

DUKE. No, no. Attend me at the garden gate.
I will be there with lover's haste—Away.
I shall behind you but a moment stay.

Exit [ATTENDANTS].

(Aside) Now, Love, assist and prosper my design,
And I no power will deify like thine.
I will Umira ravish from her cell,
And what she does deny to yield, compel.

To him the DUCHESS.

Madame, 'tis late. You should retire to rest,
The night grows old—

DUCHESS. My soul is so oppressed,
And storm'd with trouble I no rest can take.
I feeling griefs that keep me still awake.

DUKE. This is no time for story or I would
Oblige you, Isabella, to unfold
The cause of your affliction, but I now
Have only time to say good night to you.

Exit.

DUCHESS. It shall no more my shame or torment be
That he's so cold in his respect to me,
Since I'll by my revenge his love destroy,
And her he so much wishes to enjoy.
What is't could make me guilty of that sin,
But the desire I have to punish him,
Which I by no design can ever do,
But this alone, and this I will pursue.

Exit.

Enter STATENOR and floradine.

STATENOR. Now, floradine, what does Merantha say?

floradine. I did, my Lord, implicitly obey
What you commanded, but all I could move
Could not induce her to receive your love.

STATENOR. In vain I must attempt if thou wantest force,
To conquer her fair breast into remorse.
Ah, floradine! What will become of me,
Since she so pitiless resolves to be—

Enter PAGE.

PAGE. Lord, Cleophon's within, and bade me say
That he must speak with you without delay.

STATENOR. He shall—

Exit STATENOR and PAGE.

floradine gazes after STATENOR.

floradine. My eyes have lost him. Why should I
His absence for a trivial moment sigh,
Or be so vain to think I ever part
With him that constantly dwells in my heart.
But 'tis my soul, not eye, that hath him there.
Yet both enjoy him, when he does appear—
Ah Love! How much unjust art thou to me,
Making my love at best my misery—

Exit.

Enter STATENOR, CLEOPHON.

STATENOR. Dear Cleophon, must my Umira die?
Who is't designs this act of cruelty?

CLEOPHON. Trasilius, to Franciscus my try'd friend,
Freely discourses all he does intend.
The Duchess' eyes have set his soul on fire.
And he performs this crime at her desire.
That lustful villain must Umira kill
This night. Friend, it is Isabella's will.
Her nature cannot such a rival brook.
And what's as bad, the intention of the Duke
Is this black evening, in a strange disguise,
With others your fair sister to surprise,
And force from her the love which she denies.
Therefore make haste and let us to the urn,
Lest a delay produce us cause to mourn.

STATENOR. By heaven, I will but arm myself—Away.
I'll throw my vengeance 'mongst them all ere day.

Exit hastily.

The hearse discovering MERANTHA sleeping at one end of it, and UMIRA at the other. TRASILIUS, disguised, with his sword drawn.

TRASILIUS. I cannot look upon that face and do
The monstrous act that love does force me to.

He turns aside and kills UMIRA.

UMIRA. Oh—What art thou that hast a life destroyed,
That ne'er by me was perfectly enjoyed?
Oh! Oh!

MERANTHA wakes and runs to her.

Enter CLEOPHON.

CLEOPHON. Ha! Thou prodigious slave. What hast thou done?
Trasilius, stay! In vain thou strivest to shun
That justice, which thou must receive from me.

TRASILIUS. Since I'm discovered, I'll not fly from thee.

They fight.

Enter STATENOR. TRASILIUS falls.

STATENOR. Hold, Cleophon—Permit my sword to do
What much more nearly me concerns than you.

CLEOPHON. I've paid him, friend, what to his crime was due.

Enter the DUKE with three or four disguised.

STATENOR. More conspirators against Innocence.

STATENOR runs at the DUKE, defends himself and fights, and CLEOPHON beats off the Duke's party.

STATENOR kills the DUKE and falls himself.

STATENOR. Best Cleophon, do not remove me hence.
I must retire into death, nature's shade.
Let me by noble Philammon be laid.
Merantha then will o're my ashes grieve.
And I shall be more blessed than all that live.

MERANTHA. Merantha has so short a time to stay
In this bad world that, Sir, she shall not pay
Ought to your memory when you are dead—
Is not Umira to Elysium fled?
Her glorious soul has touched that shore ere this,
Where faithful lovers live in endless bliss,
And it were sin for me to stay behind.

Merantha will be just as she was kind,
Who vowed if Heaven first summoned me away,
That after she would not a moment stay.
Dear virgin, as thy love was great to me,
Thus I express, mine was no less to thee.

Kills herself.

STATENOR. Unjust in this—You might have given me leave
First to have gone to my expecting grave.

MERANTHA. No. Love and friendship both do hasten me
To their enjoyment, to eternity.

CLEOPHON. Oh my dear sister—that you had impressed
The wound on mine you have on your own breast.

MERANTHA. In wishing that, against my fame you sin.
Now, Statenor, you have my justice seen.
And when you have expired, you may unfold
To my Umira in the other world,
What for her sake, Merantha here did do.
The story will be handsomest told by you.
Brother, you'll not deny if you are just,
To mix our ashes with Philammon's dust.

Dies.

STATENOR. Oh, she is gone! My soul is on the wing
To follow her—Life flows out at this spring.

The DUKE groans.

What's he afflicted with approaching death
That does in such sad sighs resign his breath?

CLEOPHON pulls off [the Duke's] false beard.

CLEOPHON. It is the Duke. What tragedy is here?
I am surprised with horror and with fear.

STATENOR. He fell a sacrifice to his own lust.
The gods are merciful—but they are just.
(To CLEOPHON) That justice I cannot survive to do
On Isabella must be done by you.

Enter floradine, who stands amazed.

How much obliged unto my fate am I,
Dear Youth, that lets me see thee ere I die.
All that in Tuscany was ere called mine
Possess, for I do frankly make it thine.

floradine. Swiftly it shall be shown by what I do
That I this bounty prize not without you.
What you have given I never must enjoy.
Since you are not, what should I do but die.
Whilst you do leave the world, I will not stay.
Duty and love, Sir, make me lead the way.

Stabs himself.

Statenor. Hold! Cruel floradine, what hast thou done?
Thy death gives me more torment than my own.

Cleophon. I'm so astonished at his gallantry
That wonder above grief possesseth me.

Statenor. My hasty soul does stay to wonder too
What Roman could a greater action do?[44]

floaradine. Did I not more, Sir, for the love of you
When I transformed myself from what I am?
And though a maid, in show a youth became.
And the stolen name of floradine did own,
Where I for Erasila was not known,
And did your page become, that so I might
The blessing have to be within your sight,
Whom I did love more than the world does light,
And on that score, I did my sex abuse.
Let Love that made me err, the fault excuse.

Statenor starts up.

Statenor. Ha! Erasila—why would you conceal
This truth which much too late you now reveal?
Since I cannot survive to pay to you
What to a love so great as thine is due.

44. It was a Roman custom to commit suicide rather than tarnish one's reputation with an ignoble survival after the death of comrades. Cf. Shakespeare's *Macbeth*: "Why should I play the Roman fool and die / On mine own sword?" (5.8.1–2).

floradine. Could you have loved me, Sir?

STATENOR. Oh! Had you tried
Whilst I the sweetness of a life enjoyed?
That love I did to fair Merantha vow,
In justice must be Erasila's now.
And this request I make in my last breath,
That she would give herself to me in death.
I in the other world with better right
May challenge thee if here we do unite,
And link our souls. Thus I my spirit resign.

Kisses her.

floradine. And in your bosom, I do give up mine.

She dies.

He takes her in his arms.

STATENOR. Oh, she is gone. But I will her pursue.
Farewell dear Cle—o—phon . . .

He dies.

CLEOPHON. Heavens! He dies too
Where shall I weep? I do not yet perceive
O're which of these I should begin to grieve.
Each of these famous lovers I avow
Deserves more tears than Cleophon knows how
To pay their losses. To the other two,
There is from me some little sorrow due.
S:rH: Herbert X For it is fit,
S:rH: Herbert X All that so sin, should punished be for it.[45]

Enter in their nightgowns with torches EUMENUS, CLEON, FRANCISCUS, and the Duke's party.

EUMENUS. Heavens! Much more has happened than we feared.
And all is short of truth, which these declared.

45. The cross marks beside lines 242 and 243 suggest that the Master of the Revels again found something to object to here. Perhaps, given that the Duke has just been "punished" by death, these lines make too close an allusion to Charles II's well-known amorous activities.

CLEON. The Duke, Trasilius, Statenor, being dead,
The Tuscan wreath,[46] Sir, must impale your head.

CLEOPHON. 'Tis true, my Lords, as I perceive you just.
I hope you will believe I should, and must.

Whispers [to] FRANCISCUS.

FRANCISCUS. Upon my life, my Lord, it shall be done.
Your help, to carry these to the next room.

The ATTENDANTS help off with the dead bodies.

CLEOPHON. (To the LORDS) Your patience in the cloister I desire
Whilst but a few short minutes I retire.

Exit severally.

The DUCHESS discovered on a couch in a rich nightdress. Soft music and a song within.

Song ended. One knocks.

DUCHESS. Who's there? Trasilius?

CLEOPHON. No. It is not he.

He enters.

Madame, the Duke has sent for you by me.

DUCHESS. (Aside) I fear my friend in what he undertook,
In the attempt discovered to the Duke.
Let what will happen, I'll plead innocent.
I cannot rest 'till I do know th'event.
Though 'tis at an odd hour, Sir, I will go.

CLEOPHON. Madame, I readily attend on you.

Exit both.

The curtain is let fall. Solemn music awhile as it is drawn up again. The music ceases. At one door, enter CLEOPHON and the DUCHESS. At the other, the LORDS.

46. A representation of a crown, implying that Cleophon will be the new duke.

DUCHESS. Inform me, Sir, why you have brought me here.

CLEOPHON. That you shall guess by those which now appear.

The scene opens discovering UMIRA, MERANTHA, and ERASILA like a woman in white—with sparkling wreaths or coronets upon their heads—dead on a couch. STATENOR's head placed on ERASILA's lap. At the other side [of] the scene, TRASILIUS and the DUKE are laid.

CLEOPHON. (To the LORDS) I said you should be satisfied by me
What authored this unheard of tragedy.

DUCHESS. What fatal objects do my sense surprise,
Showing my soul strange horrors through my eyes.
Death never knew a triumph like to this—

CLEOPHON. This does excel even all the victories
He ever gained o're nature heretofore.
And of his ill success must still deplore.
Yet there's not one which he did here subdue,
But owes a ruin less to him, than you.
You were the cause of all the spoils you see,
For which, Lady, you should strangely punished be.
No punishment indeed can reach your crime.
You would confess it if you knew your sin.
But you're half-ignorant of what you've done.
Although the least you meant, you'll sigh to own,
And if you have a soul, but you have none.

She addresses herself to speak. He interrupts her.

All you can urge can ne'er my spirit move,
That I should live to punish what I love.
(Aside) Oh, had her mind resembled but her face.

ISABELLA kneels.

ISABELLA. If you have justice, let me quit this place.
Send me to death—

CLEOPHON. No, Madame, you shall live.
And since by law I must your sentence give,
For two respects it shall be less severe,
Than if that you another person were.
The first is, you my prince's widow are.

The last, I loved you once, I must declare.
But you were false to him and false to me.
Go and betake you to a monast'ry.
And weep your life in penitence away.
And an example be to all that may
Be faithless like you. You, my Lord, must see
My will performed, in what I now decree.

EUMENUS. I shall, my gracious Lord—

CLEOPHON. I shall to you
Show a sufficient cause for what I do.

CLEOPHON turns to the dead bodies and looks upon them.

CLEOPHON. Oh glorious maids, who can express your worth,
Or what is he can limn your progress forth?
Rare miracles of faith and constancy,
But the world[47] shall weep your fates with me.
Umira and Merantha in this tomb
Must be interred with noble Philammon.
But Erasila and her Statenor,
Whose losses all brave lovers must deplore,
Shall in a monument enclosed be,
That I will build up to their memory.

Turns to the DUCHESS.

For the Duke's funeral, we will prepare.
It shall be solemnized with pomp and care.
And your Trasilius shall have what is due
To his high birth, although he sinned for you.
Go wash your blemished soul in contrite tears.
'Till it grows white, as now it black appears.
May you a penitential convert die,
Though you must still survive to infamy.
But fame to this and after ages shall
The faithful virgins ever more extoll.

Exeunt omnes.

FINIS

47. The manuscript here reads, "But the would world." As it seems the "would" is an error, it has simply been dropped here.

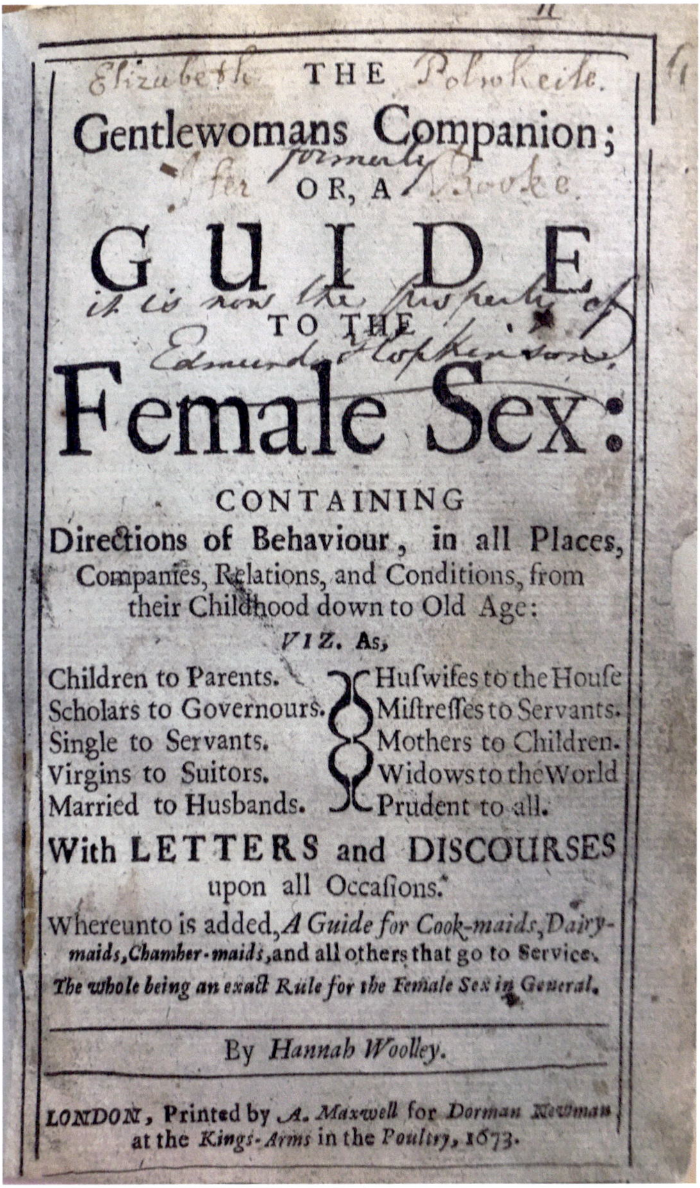

THE

Gentlewomans Companion;

OR, A

GUIDE

TO THE

Female Sex:

CONTAINING

Directions of Behaviour, in all Places, Companies, Relations, and Conditions, from their Childhood down to Old Age:

VIZ. As,

Children to Parents.	Husfwifes to the House
Scholars to Governours.	Miftreffes to Servants.
Single to Servants.	Mothers to Children.
Virgins to Suitors.	Widows to the World
Married to Husbands.	Prudent to all.

With LETTERS and DISCOURSES upon all Occafions.

Whereunto is added, *A Guide for Cook-maids, Dairy-maids, Chamber-maids*, and all others that go to Service.

The whole being an exact Rule for the Female Sex in General.

By *Hannah Woolley.*

LONDON, Printed by *A. Maxwell* for *Dorman Newman* at the *Kings-Arms* in the *Poultry*, 1673.

Figure 7. Title page of *The Gentlewomans Companion; or, A Guide to the Female Sex*, with signature "Elizabeth Polwheile Her Booke." British Library, London. BL C.194.a.1455.

ON HIS

ROYAL HIGHNESS

His Expedition againſt the DUTCH.

By Mrs. E. P.

PRoud Hogen, Mogen's, we will make you bow,
Have at you, greaſy Butter Boxes now,
Brave *York* once more againſt you does advance,
And in him more then all the Power of *France*;
'T oppoſe him is in vain, all you can do,
Is nothing, his name's enough to Conquer you.
But when in Perſon he vouchſafes to appear
Prepare to think your day of Doom is near.
That glorious *Hero*, never Arms put on
But he made Victory her ſelf his own;
Who ſtill has wav'd her white Plume o're his head,
And now to vanquiſh you, by her is lead.
Though 'tis a ſhame, (that worthy) ſhould perſue,
Honour unto ſuch Savage Bores as you.
But you (this never dying fame) ſhall know,
What in his Countreys quarrel he dare do.
Preſumptuous Villains, could you find out none,
But *England's* King, to uſe your jeſts upon?
Slaves, you e're long ſhall know, none was leſs fit,
To be a Subject for your ſcurvy wit.
(But *York* in whoſe Illuſtrious name are charms,
That Cowards hearts ev'n with pure courage warms
And does infuſe new Soul in ev'ry man,
With much more vigour then dull Brandy can.)
Will puniſh each affront that you have done
To your inevitable deſtruction.
Hee'l make you curſe the time, you Pictures drew
And draw ſome of ye, nay and hang you too.
Full of your Fate, he's with our Fleet ſet forth,
With ſuch a noble train of Engliſh youth.
That when thoſe matchleſs numbers, you ſhall veiw,
You'l think the world is come to Conquer you.
Methinks I hear the injur'd Spirits call
(For Vengeance) that did at *Amboyna* fall.
Victims, to your unheard of Cruelty,
(To thoſe) that for them will revenged be.
Their Souls do hover o're our Ships, and ſeem
To promiſe Conqueſt both to us and them.
Our Fleet like to a moving Realm, I ſee
In Tryumph on the boſome of the Sea.
Which bears it proudly, being a Jem of more
(Worth) then ſh' has worn upon her breſt before.
The Sea-gods wait upon it all along,
And thouſand water-Nymphs about it throng.
The waves their Royal burden gently court,
And all the wind's, with the calm Ocean ſport.
Tithon gives *Thetis* leave, to entertain
In all her charmes, our Gallants on the Mayn.
And's pleas'd in ſpight of age and jealouſie,
They ſhall on his young Mrs. Boſome lye.
Each Power to us, does kind preſages give
That as our cauſe is juſt, ſo we ſhall thrive.
Wit is too like a common friend, indeed,
VVho ſtill forſakes us when we have moſt need.
Or ſomewhat more ſhould be by me expreſt,
But let our Canons ſpeak to you the reſt.
And tell you to your ruines you muſt dye
T'apeaſe the wrath of Anger'd Majeſty.

FINIS.

With Allowance.

Printed in the Year, 1672.

Figure 8. "On His Royal Highness: His Expedition against the Dutch." Broadside ballad, 1672. © British Library Board. General Reference Collection C.20.f.5.(98). Image produced by ProQuest as part of *Early English Books Online*. www.proquest.com. Image published with the permission of ProQuest. Further reproduction is prohibited without permission.

Bibliography

Primary Sources

Manuscripts

Polewheele, Elnora. "Baptismal Record." Staffordshire Record Office. D1364/1/1. St. Michael and All Angels, Tettenhall Regis, Parish Register, 1643.

Polewheele, William. "Will of William Polewheele of Perton, Staffordshire." 23 June 1610. The National Archives of the UK (TNA). PROB 11/115/638. https://discovery.nationalarchives.gov.uk/details/r/D916043.

Polwheele, E. *The Faithful Virgins*. Bodleian Library, MS. Rawl. poet. 195, fols. 49–78.

Polwhele, E. *The Frolicks*. Cornell University Library, Archives 4600 Bd. MS 143 (formerly MSS Bd. Rare P P77).

Printed Items

Behn, Aphra. *The Works of Aphra Behn*. Vol. 5. Edited by Janet Todd. London: William Pickering, 1996.

Evelyn, John. *The Diary of John Evelyn*. Vol. 1. Edited by William Bray. New York: M. Walter Dunne, 1901.

Flecknoe, Richard. "A Short Discourse of the English Stage." In *Love's Kingdom*. London: R. Flecknoe, 1664.

Howard, Robert. *Four New Plays*. London: Henry Herringman, 1665.

Pepys, Samuel. *The Diary of Samuel Pepys*. Vol. 2, *1661*. Edited by Robert C. Latham and William Matthews. London: G. Bell & Sons, 1970.

Polwhele, E. *The Frolicks; or, The Lawyer Cheated (1671)*. Edited by Judith Milhous and Robert D. Hume. Ithaca, NY: Cornell University Press, 1977.

Polwhele, Elizabeth. "On His Royal Highness: His Expedition against the Dutch." In *Early Modern Women Poets: An Anthology*. Edited by Jane Stevenson and Peter Davidson, 408–11. Oxford: Oxford University Press, 2006.

Woolley, Hannah. *The Gentlewomans Companion; or, A Guide to the Female Sex*. London: A. Maxwell for Dorman Newman, 1673.

Secondary Sources

Bate, Jonathan, and Russell Jackson, eds. *Shakespeare: An Illustrated Stage History*. Oxford: Oxford University Press, 1996.

Bawcutt, N. W. *The Control and Censorship of Caroline Drama: The Records of Sir Henry Herbert, Master of the Revels, 1623–73*. Oxford: Clarendon Press, 1996.

Bold, John. "Webb, John (1611–1672)." In *Oxford Dictionary of National Biography*, edited by Lawrence Goldman. Oxford: Oxford University Press, 2004. https://doi.org/10.1093/ref:odnb/28922.

Boswell, Eleanore. *The Restoration Court Stage, 1660–1702: With a Particular Account of the Production of Calisto*. 1932. Reprint, New York: Barnes and Noble, 1966.

Dutton, Richard. "Herbert, Sir Henry (*bap*. 1594, *d*. 1673)." In *Oxford Dictionary of National Biography*, edited by Lawrence Golden. Oxford: Oxford University Press, 2004. https://doi.org/10.1093/ref:odnb/13029.

Edmond, Mary. "Davenant [D'Avenant], Sir William (1606–1668)." In *Oxford Dictionary of National Biography*, edited by Lawrence Goldman. Oxford: Oxford University Press, 2004. https://doi.org/10.1093/ref:odnb/7197.

Findlay, Alison. "Licensed to Thrill: Early Restoration Drama." In *Women and Dramatic Production, 1550–1700*, edited by Alison Findlay and Stephanie Hodgson-Wright, with Gweno Williams, 123–50. New York: Routledge, 2000.

Fisk, Deborah Payne, ed. *The Cambridge Companion to Restoration Theatre*. Cambridge: Cambridge University Press, 2000.

Gallagher, Catherine. "Who Was That Masked Woman? The Prostitute and the Playwright in the Comedies of Aphra Behn." *Women's Studies* 15, no. 1–3 (1988): 23–42. https://doi.org/10.1080/00497878.1988.9978715.

Harbage, Alfred, ed. *Annals of English Drama, 975–1700*. 2nd ed. Revised by S. Schoenbaum. London: Methuen, 1964.

Heawood, Edward, ed. *Watermarks, Mainly of the 17th and 18th Centuries*. Hilversum, Holland: Paper Publications Society, 1950.

Howe, Elizabeth. *The First English Actresses: Women and Drama, 1660–1700*. Cambridge: Cambridge University Press, 1992.

Hughes, Derek. *English Drama, 1660–1700*. Oxford: Clarendon Press, 1996.

———. "Public Drama." In *The Cambridge Companion to Early Modern Women's Writing*, edited by Laura Lunger Knoppers, 260–71. Cambridge: Cambridge University Press, 2009.

———. *The Theatre of Aphra Behn*. Hampshire: Palgrave, 1988.

Hume, Robert D. *The Development of English Drama in the Late Seventeenth Century*. Oxford: Clarendon Press, 1976.

———. "Theatre Performance Records in London, 1660–1705." *The Review of English Studies* 67, no. 280 (June 2016): 468–95. https://doi.org/10.1093/res/hgv128.

Hurley, Ann Hollinshead. "Editing the Unknown: Writing the Introduction to Two Plays by E. Polwhele." In *Women Editing/Editing Women: Early Modern*

Women Writers and the New Textualism, edited by Ann Hollinshead Hurley and Chanita Goodblatt, 189–202. Cambridge: Cambridge Scholars Press, 2009.

Hutton, Ronald. *Charles the Second: King of England, Scotland, and Ireland*. Oxford: Clarendon Press, 1989.

Keenan, Tim. *Restoration Staging, 1660–74*. London: Routledge, 2017.

Knoppers, Laura Lunger. "Introduction: Critical Framework and Issues." In *The Cambridge Companion to Early Modern Women's Writing*, edited by Laura Lunger Knoppers, 1–18. Cambridge: Cambridge University Press, 2009.

Langhans, Edward A. "The Post-1660 Theatres as Performance Spaces." In *A Companion to Restoration Drama*, edited by Susan J. Owen, 3–18. Oxford: Blackwell, 2001.

———. "Theatre." In *The Cambridge Companion to English Restoration Theatre*, edited by Deborah Payne Fisk, 1–18. Cambridge: Cambridge University Press, 2000.

Larminie, Vivienne M. *Wealth, Kinship, and Culture: The Seventeenth-Century Newdigates of Arbury and Their World*. Woodbridge, Suffolk: Boydell Press, 1995.

Leacroft, Richard. *The Development of the English Playhouse*. Ithaca, NY: Cornell University Press, 1973.

Lewcock, Dawn. *Aphra Behn Stages the Social Scene in the Restoration Theatre*. Amherst, NY: Cambria Press, 2008.

———. *Sir William Davenant, the Court Masque, and the English Seventeenth-Century Scenic Stage, c. 1605–c. 1700*. Amherst, NY: Cambria Press, 2008.

Madan, Falconer, ed. *A Summary Catalogue of Western Manuscripts in the Bodleian Library at Oxford*. Vol. 3, *Collections Received During the 18th Century*. Oxford: Clarendon Press, 1895.

Maguire, Nancy Klein. *Regicide and Restoration: English Tragicomedy, 1660–1671*. Cambridge: Cambridge University Press, 1992.

Mambretti, Catherine Cole. "Orinda on the Restoration Stage." *Comparative Literature* 37, no. 3 (Summer 1985): 233–51. https://doi.org/10.2307/1771080.

Milhous, Judith. "Polewheele, E. (165l?–1691?)." In *Oxford Dictionary of National Biography*, edited by Lawrence Goldman. Oxford: Oxford University Press, 2004. https://doi.org/10.1093/ref:odnb/45820.

Milhous, Judith, and Robert D. Hume. Introduction to *The Frolicks; or, The Lawyer Cheated (1671)*, by E. Polwhele, 13–54. Ithaca, NY: Cornell University Press, 1977.

———. *Producible Interpretation: Eight English Plays 1675–1707*. Carbondale: Southern Illinois University Press, 1985.

———, eds. *A Register of English Theatrical Documents, 1660–1737*. Vol. 1. Carbondale: Southern Illinois University Press, 1991.

Newman, John. "Jones, Inigo (1573–1652)." In *Oxford Dictionary of National Biography*, edited by Lawrence Goldman. Oxford: Oxford University Press, 2004. https://doi.org/10.1093/ref:odnb/15017.

Orgel, Stephen, and Roy C. Strong. *Inigo Jones: The Theatre of the Stuart Court*. 2 vols. London: Sotheby Parke Bernet; Berkeley: University of California Press, 1973.

Pearson, Jacqueline. *The Prostituted Muse: Images of Women and Women Dramatists, 1642–1737*. New York: St. Martin's Press, 1988.

Southern, Richard. *Changeable Scenery: Its Origins and Development in the British Theatre*. London: Faber and Faber, 1952.

Summers, Montague. *The Playhouse of Pepys*. 1935. Reprint, New York: Humanities Press, 1964.

Van Lennep, William, Emmett L. Avery, and Arthur H. Scouten, eds. *The London Stage, 1660–1800*. Part 1, *1600–1700*. Carbondale: Southern Illinois University Press, 1965.

Wall, Wendy. *The Imprint of Gender: Authority and Publication in the English Renaissance*. Ithaca, NY: Cornell University Press, 1993.

Index

Page numbers in italics refer to figures.

The Other Voice in Early Modern Europe: The Toronto Series

Series Titles

MADRE MARÍA ROSA
Journey of Five Capuchin Nuns
Edited and translated by Sarah E. Owens
Volume 1, 2009

GIOVAN BATTISTA ANDREINI
Love in the Mirror: *A Bilingual Edition*
Edited and translated by Jon R. Snyder
Volume 2, 2009

RAYMOND DE SABANAC AND SIMONE ZANACCHI
Two Women of the Great Schism: The Revelations *of Constance de Rabastens by Raymond de Sabanac and* Life of the Blessed Ursulina of Parma *by Simone Zanacchi*
Edited and translated by Renate Blumenfeld-Kosinski and Bruce L. Venarde
Volume 3, 2010

OLIVA SABUCO DE NANTES BARRERA
The True Medicine
Edited and translated by Gianna Pomata
Volume 4, 2010

LOUISE-GENEVIÈVE GILLOT DE SAINCTONGE
Dramatizing Dido, Circe, and Griselda
Edited and translated by Janet Levarie Smarr
Volume 5, 2010

PERNETTE DU GUILLET
Complete Poems: A Bilingual Edition
Edited with introduction and notes by Karen Simroth James
Poems translated by Marta Rijn Finch
Volume 6, 2010

ANTONIA PULCI
Saints' Lives and Bible Stories for the Stage: A Bilingual Edition
Edited by Elissa B. Weaver
Translated by James Wyatt Cook
Volume 7, 2010

VALERIA MIANI
Celinda, A Tragedy: *A Bilingual Edition*
Edited with an introduction by Valeria Finucci
Translated by Julia Kisacky
Annotated by Valeria Finucci and Julia Kisacky
Volume 8, 2010

Enchanted Eloquence: Fairy Tales by Seventeenth-Century French Women Writers
Edited and translated by Lewis C. Seifert and Domna C. Stanton
Volume 9, 2010

Gottfried Wilhelm Leibniz, Sophie, Electress of Hanover and Queen Sophie Charlotte of Prussia
Leibniz and the Two Sophies: The Philosophical Correspondence
Edited and translated by Lloyd Strickland
Volume 10, 2011

In Dialogue with the Other Voice in Sixteenth-Century Italy: Literary and Social Contexts for Women's Writing
Edited by Julie D. Campbell and Maria Galli Stampino
Volume 11, 2011

Sister Giustina Niccolini
The Chronicle of Le Murate
Edited and translated by Saundra Weddle
Volume 12, 2011

Liubov Krichevskaya
No Good without Reward: Selected Writings: A Bilingual Edition
Edited and translated by Brian James Baer
Volume 13, 2011

Elizabeth Cooke Hoby Russell
The Writings of an English Sappho
Edited by Patricia Phillippy
With translations from Greek and Latin by Jaime Goodrich
Volume 14, 2011

Lucrezia Marinella
Exhortations to Women and to Others If They Please
Edited and translated by Laura Benedetti
Volume 15, 2012

Margherita Datini
Letters to Francesco Datini
Translated by Carolyn James and Antonio Pagliaro
Volume 16, 2012

Delarivier Manley and Mary Pix
English Women Staging Islam, 1696–1707
Edited and introduced by Bernadette Andrea
Volume 17, 2012

Cecilia del Nacimiento
Journeys of a Mystic Soul in Poetry and Prose
Introduction and prose translations by Kevin Donnelly
Poetry translations by Sandra Sider
Volume 18, 2012

Lady Margaret Douglas and Others
The Devonshire Manuscript: A Women's Book of Courtly Poetry
Edited and introduced by Elizabeth Heale
Volume 19, 2012

Arcangela Tarabotti
Letters Familiar and Formal
Edited and translated by Meredith K. Ray and Lynn Lara Westwater
Volume 20, 2012

Pere Torrellas and Juan de Flores
Three Spanish Querelle *Texts:* Grisel and Mirabella, The Slander against Women, *and* The Defense of Ladies against Slanderers: *A Bilingual Edition and Study*
Edited and translated by Emily C. Francomano
Volume 21, 2013

Barbara Torelli Benedetti
Partenia, a Pastoral Play: *A Bilingual Edition*
Edited and translated by Lisa Sampson and Barbara Burgess-Van Aken
Volume 22, 2013

François Rousset, Jean Liebault, Jacques Guillemeau, Jacques Duval and Louis de Serres
Pregnancy and Birth in Early Modern France: Treatises by Caring Physicians and Surgeons (1581–1625)
Edited and translated by Valerie Worth-Stylianou
Volume 23, 2013

Mary Astell
The Christian Religion, as Professed by a Daughter of the Church of England
Edited by Jacqueline Broad
Volume 24, 2013

Sophia of Hanover
Memoirs (1630–1680)
Edited and translated by Sean Ward
Volume 25, 2013

Katherine Austen
Book M: *A London Widow's Life Writings*
Edited by Pamela S. Hammons
Volume 26, 2013

Anne Killigrew
"My Rare Wit Killing Sin": Poems of a Restoration Courtier
Edited by Margaret J. M. Ezell
Volume 27, 2013

Tullia d'Aragona and Others
The Poems and Letters of Tullia d'Aragona and Others: A Bilingual Edition
Edited and translated by Julia L. Hairston
Volume 28, 2014

Luisa de Carvajal y Mendoza
The Life and Writings of Luisa de Carvajal y Mendoza
Edited and translated by Anne J. Cruz
Volume 29, 2014

Russian Women Poets of the Eighteenth and Early Nineteenth Centuries: A Bilingual Edition
Edited and translated by Amanda Ewington
Volume 30, 2014

Jacques Du Bosc
L'Honnête Femme: The Respectable Woman in Society *and the* New Collection of Letters and Responses by Contemporary Women
Edited and translated by Sharon Diane Nell and Aurora Wolfgang
Volume 31, 2014

Lady Hester Pulter
Poems, Emblems, *and* The Unfortunate Florinda
Edited by Alice Eardley
Volume 32, 2014

Jeanne Flore
Tales and Trials of Love, Concerning Venus's Punishment of Those Who Scorn True Love and Denounce Cupid's Sovereignity: *A Bilingual Edition and Study*
Edited and translated by Kelly Digby Peebles
Poems translated by Marta Rijn Finch
Volume 33, 2014

Veronica Gambara
Complete Poems: A Bilingual Edition
Critical introduction by Molly M. Martin
Edited and translated by Molly M. Martin and Paola Ugolini
Volume 34, 2014

Catherine de Médicis and Others
Portraits of the Queen Mother: Polemics, Panegyrics, Letters
Translation and study by Leah L. Chang and Katherine Kong
Volume 35, 2014

Françoise Pascal, Marie-Catherine Desjardins, Antoinette Deshoulières, and Catherine Durand
Challenges to Traditional Authority: Plays by French Women Authors, 1650–1700
Edited and translated by Perry Gethner
Volume 36, 2015

Franciszka Urszula Radziwiłłowa
Selected Drama and Verse
Edited by Patrick John Corness and Barbara Judkowiak
Translated by Patrick John Corness
Translation Editor Aldona Zwierzyńska-Coldicott
Introduction by Barbara Judkowiak
Volume 37, 2015

Diodata Malvasia
Writings on the Sisters of San Luca and Their Miraculous Madonna
Edited and translated by Danielle Callegari and Shannon McHugh
Volume 38, 2015

Margaret Van Noort
Spiritual Writings of Sister Margaret of the Mother of God (1635–1643)
Edited by Cordula van Wyhe
Translated by Susan M. Smith
Volume 39, 2015

Giovan Francesco Straparola
The Pleasant Nights
Edited and translated by Suzanne Magnanini
Volume 40, 2015

Angélique de Saint-Jean Arnauld d'Andilly
Writings of Resistance
Edited and translated by John J. Conley, S.J.
Volume 41, 2015

Francesco Barbaro
The Wealth of Wives: A Fifteenth-Century Marriage Manual
Edited and translated by Margaret L. King
Volume 42, 2015

Jeanne d'Albret
Letters from the Queen of Navarre with an Ample Declaration
Edited and translated by Kathleen M. Llewellyn, Emily E. Thompson, and Colette H. Winn
Volume 43, 2016

Bathsua Makin and Mary More with a reply to More by Robert Whitehall
Educating English Daughters: Late Seventeenth-Century Debates
Edited by Frances Teague and Margaret J. M. Ezell
Associate Editor Jessica Walker
Volume 44, 2016

Anna Stanisławska
Orphan Girl: A Transaction, or an Account of the Entire Life of an Orphan Girl by way of Plaintful Threnodies in the Year 1685: *The Aesop Episode*
Verse translation, introduction, and commentary by Barry Keane
Volume 45, 2016

Alessandra Macinghi Strozzi
Letters to Her Sons, 1447–1470
Edited and translated by Judith Bryce
Volume 46, 2016

Mother Juana de la Cruz
Mother Juana de la Cruz, 1481–1534: Visionary Sermons
Edited by Jessica A. Boon and Ronald E. Surtz
Introductory material and notes by Jessica A. Boon
Translated by Ronald E. Surtz and Nora Weinerth
Volume 47, 2016

Claudine-Alexandrine Guérin de Tencin
Memoirs of the Count of Comminge *and* The Misfortunes of Love
Edited and translated by Jonathan Walsh
Foreword by Michel Delon
Volume 48, 2016

Feliciana Enríquez de Guzmán, Ana Caro Mallén, and Sor Marcela de San Félix
Women Playwrights of Early Modern Spain
Edited by Nieves Romero-Díaz and Lisa Vollendorf
Translated and annotated by Harley Erdman
Volume 49, 2016

Anna Trapnel
Anna Trapnel's Report and Plea; or, A Narrative of Her Journey from London into Cornwall
Edited by Hilary Hinds
Volume 50, 2016

María Vela y Cueto
Autobiography and Letters of a Spanish Nun
Edited by Susan Diane Laningham
Translated by Jane Tar
Volume 51, 2016

Christine de Pizan
The Book of the Mutability of Fortune
Edited and translated by Geri L. Smith
Volume 52, 2017

Marguerite d'Auge, Renée Burlamacchi, and Jeanne du Laurens
Sin and Salvation in Early Modern France: Three Women's Stories
Edited, and with an introduction by Colette H. Winn
Translated by Nicholas Van Handel and Colette H. Winn
Volume 53, 2017

Isabella d'Este
Selected Letters
Edited and translated by Deanna Shemek
Volume 54, 2017

Ippolita Maria Sforza
Duchess and Hostage in Renaissance Naples: Letters and Orations
Edited and translated by Diana Robin and Lynn Lara Westwater
Volume 55, 2017

Louise Bourgeois
Midwife to the Queen of France: Diverse Observations
Translated by Stephanie O'Hara
Edited by Alison Klairmont Lingo
Volume 56, 2017

Christine de Pizan
Othea's Letter to Hector
Edited and translated by Renate Blumenfeld-Kosinski and Earl Jeffrey Richards
Volume 57, 2017

Marie-Geneviève-Charlotte Thiroux d'Arconville
Selected Philosophical, Scientific, and Autobiographical Writings
Edited and translated by Julie Candler Hayes
Volume 58, 2018

Lady Mary Wroth
Pamphilia to Amphilanthus *in Manuscript and Print*
Edited by Ilona Bell
Texts by Steven W. May and Ilona Bell
Volume 59, 2017

Witness, Warning, and Prophecy: Quaker Women's Writing, 1655–1700
Edited by Teresa Feroli and Margaret Olofson Thickstun
Volume 60, 2018

Symphorien Champier
The Ship of Virtuous Ladies
Edited and translated by Todd W. Reeser
Volume 61, 2018

Isabella Andreini
Mirtilla, A Pastoral: *A Bilingual Edition*
Edited by Valeria Finucci
Translated by Julia Kisacky
Volume 62, 2018

Margherita Costa
The Buffoons, A Ridiculous Comedy: *A Bilingual Edition*
Edited and translated by Sara E. Díaz and Jessica Goethals
Volume 63, 2018

Margaret Cavendish, Duchess of Newcastle
Poems and Fancies *with* The Animal Parliament
Edited by Brandie R. Siegfried
Volume 64, 2018

Margaret Fell
Women's Speaking Justified *and Other Pamphlets*
Edited by Jane Donawerth and Rebecca M. Lush
Volume 65, 2018

Mary Wroth, Jane Cavendish, and Elizabeth Brackley
Women's Household Drama:
Loves Victorie, A Pastorall, *and* The concealed Fansyes
Edited by Marta Straznicky and Sara Mueller
Volume 66, 2018

Eleonora Fonseca Pimentel
From Arcadia to Revolution: The Neapolitan Monitor *and Other Writings*
Edited and translated by Verina R. Jones
Volume 67, 2019

Charlotte Arbaleste Duplessis-Mornay, Anne de Chaufepié, and Anne Marguerite Petit Du Noyer
The Huguenot Experience of Persecution and Exile: Three Women's Stories
Edited by Colette H. Winn
Translated by Lauren King and Colette H. Winn
Volume 68, 2019

Anne Bradstreet
Poems and Meditations
Edited by Margaret Olofson Thickstun
Volume 69, 2019

Arcangela Tarabotti
Antisatire: *In Defense of Women, against Francesco Buoninsegni*
Edited and translated by Elissa B. Weaver
Volume 70, 2020

Mary Franklin and Hannah Burton
She Being Dead Yet Speaketh: The Franklin Family Papers
Edited by Vera J. Camden
Volume 71, 2020

Lucrezia Marinella
Love Enamored and Driven Mad
Edited and translated by Janet E. Gomez and Maria Galli Stampino
Volume 72, 2020

Arcangela Tarabotti
Convent Paradise
Edited and translated by Meredith K. Ray and Lynn Lara Westwater
Volume 73, 2020

Gabrielle-Suzanne Barbot de Villeneuve
Beauty and the Beast: *The Original Story*
Edited and translated by Aurora Wolfgang
Volume 74, 2020

Flaminio Scala
The Fake Husband, A Comedy
Edited and translated by Rosalind Kerr
Volume 75, 2020

Anne Vaughan Lock
Selected Poetry, Prose, and Translations, with Contextual Materials
Edited by Susan M. Felch
Volume 76, 2021

Camilla Erculiani
Letters on Natural Philosophy: *The Scientific Correspondence of a Sixteenth-Century Pharmacist, with Related Texts*
Edited by Eleonora Carinci
Translated by Hannah Marcus
Foreword by Paula Findlen
Volume 77, 2021

Regina Salomea Pilsztynowa
My Life's Travels and Adventures: *An Eighteenth-Century Oculist in the Ottoman Empire and the European Hinterland*
Edited and translated by Władysław Roczniak
Volume 78, 2021

Christine de Pizan
The God of Love's Letter *and* The Tale of the Rose: *A Bilingual Edition*
Edited and translated by Thelma S. Fenster and Christine Reno
With Jean Gerson, "A Poem on Man and Woman." Translated from the Latin by Thomas O'Donnell
Foreword by Jocelyn Wogan-Browne
Volume 79, 2021

Marie Gigault de Bellefonds, Marquise de Villars
Letters from Spain: A Seventeenth-Century French Noblewoman at the Spanish Royal Court
Edited and translated by Nathalie Hester
Volume 80, 2021

Anna Maria van Schurman
Letters and Poems to and from Her Mentor and Other Members of Her Circle
Edited and translated by Anne R. Larsen and Steve Maiullo
Volume 81, 2021

Vittoria Colonna
Poems of Widowhood: A Bilingual Edition of the 1538 Rime
Translation and introduction by Ramie Targoff
Edited by Ramie Targoff and Troy Tower
Volume 82, 2021

Valeria Miani
Amorous Hope, A Pastoral Play: *A Bilingual Edition*
Edited and translated by Alexandra Coller
Volume 83, 2020

Madeleine de Scudéry
Lucrece and Brutus: Glory in the Land of Tender
Edited and translated by Sharon Diane Nell
Volume 84, 2021

Anna Stanisławska
One Body with Two Souls Entwined: An Epic Tale of Married Love in Seventeenth-Century Poland
Orphan Girl: The Oleśnicki Episode
Verse translation, introduction, and commentary by Barry Keane
Volume 85, 2021

Christine de Pizan
Book of the Body Politic
Edited and translated by Angus J. Kennedy
Volume 86, 2021

Anne, Lady Halkett
A True Account of My Life *and Selected* Meditations
Edited by Suzanne Trill
Volume 87, 2022

Vittoria Colonna
Selected Letters, 1523–1546: A Bilingual Edition
Edited and annotated by Veronica Copello
Translated by Abigail Brundin
Introduction by Abigail Brundin and Veronica Copello
Volume 88, 2022

Michele Savonarola
A Mother's Manual for the Women of Ferrara: *A Fifteenth-Century Guide to Pregnancy and Pediatrics*
Edited, with introduction and notes, by Gabriella Zuccolin
Translated by Martin Marafioti
Volume 89, 2022

Maria Salviati de' Medici
Selected Letters, 1514–1543
Edited and translated by Natalie R. Tomas
Volume 90, 2022

Isabella Andreini
Lovers' Debates for the Stage: *A Bilingual Edition*
Edited and translated by Pamela Allen Brown, Julie D. Campbell, and Eric Nicholson
Volume 91, 2022

Marie Guyart de l'Incarnation, Anne-Marie Fiquet Du Boccage, and Henriette-Lucie Dillon de La Tour du Pin
Far from Home in Early Modern France: Three Women's Stories
Edited and with an introduction by Colette H. Winn
Translated by Lauren King, Elizabeth Hagstrom, and Colette H. Winn
Volume 92, 2022

Marie-Catherine Le Jumel de Barneville, baronne d'Aulnoy
Travels into Spain
Edited and translated by Gabrielle M. Verdier
Volume 93, 2022

Pierre de Vaux and Sister Perrine de Baume
Two Lives of Saint Colette. *With a Selection of Letters by, to, and about Colette*
Edited and translated by Renate Blumenfeld-Kosinski
Volume 94, 2022

Dorothy Calthorpe
News from the Midell Regions *and* Calthorpe's Chapel
Edited by Julie A. Eckerle
Volume 95, 2022

Elizabeth Poole
The Prophetess and the Patriarch: The Visions of an Anti-Regicide in Seventeenth-Century England
Edited by Katharine Gillespie
Volume 96, 2023

Mary Carleton and Others
The Carleton Bigamy Trial
Edited by Megan Matchinske
Volume 97, 2023

Marie Baudoin
The Art of Childbirth:
A Seventeenth-Century Midwife's Epistolary Treatise to Doctor Vallant
A Bilingual Edition
Edited and translated by Cathy McClive
Volume 98, 2022

Marguerite Buffet
New Observations on the French Language, *with* Praises of Illustrious Learned Women
Edited and translated by Lynn S. Meskill
Volume 99, 2023

Isabella Andreini
Letters
Edited and translated by Paola De Santo and Caterina Mongiat Farina
Volume 100, 2023

Mary Carey
A Mother's Spiritual Dialogue, Meditations, and Elegies
Edited by Pamela S. Hammons
Volume 101, 2023

Isabella Whitney
Poems by a Sixteenth-Century Gentlewoman, Maid, and Servant
Edited by Shannon Miller
Volume 102, 2023

Camilla Battista da Varano
The Spiritual Life *and Other Writings*
Edited and translated by William V. Hudon
Volume 103, 2023